T0171382

There Was Always a *Cat*

Memories of My Early Life—
the Cats I've Loved and Who Have Loved Me

Beryl Walker

(nee PEREIRA)

BALBOA.
PRESS

A DIVISION OF HAY HOUSE

Balboa Press books may be ordered through booksellers or by contacting:

Balboa Press
A Division of Hay House
1663 Liberty Drive
Bloomington, IN 47403
www.balboapress.com.au
1-(877) 407-4847

ISBN: 978-1-4525-1024-8 (sc)
ISBN: 978-1-4525-1025-5 (e)

Because of the dynamic nature of the Internet, any web addresses or links contained in this book may have changed since publication and may no longer be valid. The views expressed in this work are solely those of the author and do not necessarily reflect the views of the publisher, and the publisher hereby disclaims any responsibility for them.

Printed in the United States of America

Balboa Press rev. date: 6/7/2013

Contents

To my dear family—this is for you!

For age is opportunity no less than youth itself,
though in another dress
and as the evening twilight fades away
the sky is filled with stars invisible by day

HENRY WADSWORTH LONGFELLOW
1807-1882

Preface

I do not have many memories of my very early years but I do know that with no electricity our amusements mostly involved visits to and from neighbours and relations. When we were little we stayed close to our mother, 'helping' by standing on a box to wash or dry the dishes, and handing the pegs to Mum as she was pegging out the clothes. Books were always important to my mother and while our hair was being done in the morning the old classic stories would be told again and again; The Three Little Pigs, Goldilocks and The Three Bears.

When I was very young, I desperately wanted a baby sister or brother. I didn't really mind which, just a baby, and used to entreat God night by night for one; giving Him two weeks for the baby to appear; thinking that should be plenty of time for Him to come good with my request. The trust and innocence of childhood!

I must have been aware of myself as a person with a right to opinions and ideas quite early in life. There is a photo of me at the age of two years and one month, hands clasped in front and over them draped the inevitable cat. On the back of the photo, Aunty Stell had written "Our Larrikin", so I must have been doing something to earn that sobriquet.

Further down the track there must still have been signs that I still had a will and opinions of my own as Dad used to call me his "little protestant" which invariably called forth more voluble and fervent protestations on my part that I was *not* a protestant.

Even if it did seem to my parents that I was frequently protesting about something, "agin the government"—I had a voice!

That didn't last though and, as my sister and I grew up through our mid-teens, we rarely went anywhere that we were not sitting up on the back seat of the car, going places our parents wanted to go; being shadows of them, making few decisions for ourselves and regarded by our neighbours as over-protected. Our parents loved us dearly but we did live almost cloistered lives. Those were the years my voice disappeared.

Ah well, many years have gone by and in April 2011, I saw a notice in the *Grenfell Record* advertising a workshop to be held at the library, titled "Words from the dust".

I thought, "I want to go to that!" Decisive!

My diary dated 21st April 2011 says: *"phoned library to book a place in workshop, can hardly believe that I actually did it"*.

I have a voice, albeit through a pen. You have to believe it!

★★★★

Acknowledgements

There are many to thank for their interest and help. Firstly, my daughter Jeanette and granddaughter Michelle for giving me the books that caused me to stop, think, stir up the many memories of my life and finally write something.

Those who helped by typing from my handwritten drafts—no easy task I can assure you—were daughters Alison and Kathy, granddaughter Grace, but mostly my husband George.

I was encouraged by the interest and desire to learn more displayed by our grandsons, Mitchell and Daniel, when I showed them my tea and butter ration card and identity card from 1939.

I am especially grateful to my granddaughter Diana, who has spent many hours editing and formatting the manuscript and, with Michelle, doing the publishing research.

The biggest Thank You of all should surely go to my husband of 60 years, George, who took over the task of chief planner of the meals and cook. What a gem!

The Beginning: Grace Meets Alf

In January 1922, Grace King had a holiday with Emily and Dave Graham at 'Hopefield' near Quondong Road, Grenfell.

It was decided a pleasant outing for their guest would be to visit the Pereira family, who had been neighbours some years previously when they lived at 'Green Hills'. George and Charlotte Pereira and their young family had moved to 'Spring Vale', Cowra Road, Grenfell, in 1908.

So on 20th January, which happened to be Grace's 25th birthday, off they set in the sulky: Emily—Grace's mother's cousin, her mother Eliza Durham, and Grace. The first person Grace saw on arrival was Mavis, who was sweeping the verandah.

Tennis played on their own court was part of the entertainment during the afternoon. Grace and Alfred were partners in a game of mixed doubles when one of Grace's returns hit Alfred fair and square between the shoulders—that's one way to get a man's attention! Nonetheless, Grace must have made a good impression because she was invited to stay the night, with Mavis lending her a nightgown.

Alfred did not waste much time making his move; the first letter to "Dear Miss King" was written on 6th February. So Alfred began his courtship of Grace and the first time it was "Dear Grace" was in a letter written on 1st March asking directions to her home in Temora.

His first visit there was Saturday, 11th March, coming home on Monday the 13th. He had ordered a motor bike and didn't want to attempt the trip to Temora until he was reasonably confident with it. The roads were very different then; a dust bowl in summer, and parts of it a quagmire in winter. Alfred also had quite a few problems with his Indian motor bike, sometimes seeming to have to push it as much as ride it.

Alfred and Grace during their courtship in 1922.

The Kings didn't have the telephone connected so the young couple weren't able to keep in touch that way. They did write many letters and we are fortunate to have all that were written by Alfred; the last dated a few days before their wedding in the Cowra Road Methodist Church, on the Spring Vale property.

Alfred and Grace were married on 6th June, 1923, a showery Wednesday afternoon.

I was born about noon on the 7th February, 1929 at Grenfell Cottage (Maternity) Hospital to Alfred and Grace Pereira, and named Grace Beryl Pereira. My sister Ada Elaine was exactly two-and-a-half-years older. Mothers used to stay in hospital longer then and I don't know how many days old I was when Elaine was brought in to meet her new sister. I have been told she asked, "Can I nurse her?" and was told "No", so she tried, "Can I touch her little hand?" and was told "Yes, you may touch her little hand".

The new family.

That was the beginning of our lives together and we always were good friends, doing just about everything together until I married George.

I was close to, if not a nine-pound baby, and the auburn tints in my hair soon began to show. I was called Grace or Gracie for the first few months of my life, but with lots of family members around, Mum and I were beginning to be called Big Grace and Little Grace, so I became Beryl, my second name.

My sister Elaine, soon after being born, was being carried by a sister up to the main hospital for the night, which was apparently the custom then, when the sister fell over a COW. I can't top that! I also couldn't top her in the excitement her arrival caused among the Temora relations. Many letters arrived begging for more and more information about the baby's looks and suggesting possible names. Aunty Dot liked Joy, Alice suggested Hilda, and Uncle George, who at the age of eighteen was an opera lover, wanted Carmen Delores. It evidently remained his favourite because when his and Aunty Hazel's first daughter arrived on the 4th August, 1939, that was the name she was given. (Carmen married Bradley Boyden and their second daughter Sally Anne Boyden became very well-known as a member of Johnny Young's Young Talent Time. She went on to have a very successful career in the entertainment industry.)

In a letter written by Aunty Stella just after Elaine was born she wrote *"We all rather like Elaine but it would be nice if you could work one of Mum's names in—Marie or Beanie is pretty—especially if the baby has blue eyes and black hair. We are all hoping it will stay black, and also that it will be curly."*

This made me think that my grandmother, Ada Maria Beanie King had black hair and blue eyes. Two of her children, Stella and George did. Our parents decided to call my sister Ada Elaine and later in life she was often called by both names.

I was baptised in the Cowra Road Church on the 17th March, 1929 by the Reverend E.W. Hyde and presented with a New Testament. I wore the Starr heirloom christening gown which had been worn by my grandmother, Charlotte Pereira nee Starr, also my father and all his brothers and sisters with the exception of the twins, Ruby and Pearl. It is in my care now and, as Grandma was born in 1873, it would be about 140 years old.

There was always a cat, it seems, playing an important role in my life.

We have a photograph taken at my sister's 4th birthday celebration where she is seated in the centre, our friend Margaret Hughes on one side nursing our big black cat and I am standing on the other side having just decided to get the cat back. I was just 18 months old. His name was Peter, a big, black, very dignified cat, sometimes called by my Mother 'The Colonel' because of his deportment. He was a mighty hunter but became old and just disappeared. Dad was sad because he respected Peter and would have liked to have given him an honourable burial. Another was Tibbins, a nice but not exceptional black cat with a white muzzle and bib.

We lived almost twelve miles out of town on a creek so lots of people seemed to think it was a suitable place to dump unwanted cats. Many cats came over the years hoping for a home. One was a black Persian whose fur was all matted and needing lots of care. Dad called her Gladys because he said she was so glad she had found us!

Elaine and I both had dolls; Elaine's favourite she named Hazel and the story is told that Elaine once said, "When I go to heaven the Angel can carry my suitcase but *I'm going to carry Hazel!*" My special doll was Doris Ruth, a brown-eyed porcelain beauty, sleeping, jointed arms and legs, but cats were what really filled my day and my heart with contentment.

Elaine and I with our dolls.

Fortunately I do not remember details of them, but I had two serious illnesses while still very young. The first was severe gastroenteritis, from which both Elaine and I suffered. It was caused by a snake getting into the well, which was our water supply, and dying there. Poor Mum and Dad; the doctor told them, "They are very ill, they could die." I can remember once the sensation of being in a long, long black tunnel being drawn against my will; inexorably further and further down. Was that a near death experience, or just a child's nightmare? I do not know.

The other illness was whooping cough, and that was the reason my starting school was delayed. The Doctor thought my heart may have been affected, and Elaine and I had to pedal our bikes three miles to school and of course, the same back again in the afternoon.

We didn't get pocket money to spend as we chose. In the Depression there wasn't money for that but sometimes Mum had made some lovely honeycomb or almond toffee during the afternoon and we would have some of that. Until things got better, Sao and wheatmeal biscuits bought bulk by weight were pretty much the only 'bought' biscuits we had and I saw them as decidedly boring.

So, when we were in our teens and Mum decided we should have our eyes tested by Doctor Bono, who rented a room upstairs in the Royal Hotel, my chance came. Perhaps we had been kept waiting and became hungry because Mum gave Elaine and I money to go to Jack Stiff's grocery store nearby and buy some biscuits. Mum nearly died when we came back with not one but TWO packets of Arnotts cream-filled biscuits.

The Creek

Bungalong Creek was right alongside our orchard and there was one part of the creek we were forbidden to go near. Being good children, we obeyed. It was a deeper hole north east from 'Big Tree'. We had been told that one hot day not long after my parents were married, they were cooling off in this part of the creek with a few friends, splashing around and enjoying themselves. Suddenly, my Mother shrieked, and shook her left hand vigorously as a leech was attached to it. But then she realised her gold wedding ring was gone. Poor Mum, naturally, was distraught and although Dad sifted through bucket after bucket of sand and soil the ring was never found. Another ring was bought and it is now on my finger next to my own wedding ring.

Swaggies

The Depression and I arrived about the same time. We became aware of the number of homeless men walking the roads, hoping for work or at least something to eat. Their swags held all they possessed, rolled up and strapped in a grey blanket, over the shoulder and down the back, a blackened billy can hanging off the side. Mum would find some bread, tea, sugar or fruit in season—something they could carry. Mum used to make our own bread in those years so it would depend on just what was available at any particular time. Some of the men had made articles that they hoped to sell for a little money, often made of wire—a cake cooler, for example. I have one, in a box of mementoes from bygone days. Often the Swaggie would offer to cut some wood as recompense for what he had received.

Temora

Our visits to Temora were mostly for weekends, sometimes longer, perhaps two or three times a year. If there was sickness or need Mum would stay on and Dad, Elaine and I would return home for work or school.

One of my memories of visits to Temora is of the Play Box kept in the laundry of my Mother's old home. Mother had three younger sisters, bright young flappers in the 1920's, especially the youngest, Aunty Dot, and this box was filled with some of their leftovers, things we definitely didn't have access to at home. There were high-heeled shoes, evening dresses and bags, hair rollers, jewellery, make up etc. On visits there, we would make a beeline for these delights and would dress up, tottering around in high heels and doubtless too much lipstick, hoping to be admired.

I have had in my possession since Elaine died, a coffee-coloured net dress which I think must have originated from Temora. It is sleeveless, has a scooped neckline and two scalloped-edged tiers in the skirt of plain net and needlerun lace embroidered with coffee silk. The centre of some of the flowers are embroidered with purple, gold and deep pink rose. The midriff area was needlerun lace too, in just coffee; gorgeous but one did need a suitable slip!

On a visit to Temora relations once when Elaine and I were about nine and seven, the subject of going to Sunday School was brought up. It didn't meet with much approval as we would not know anyone there or what to do.

Mum used some emotional blackmail on us: "This is where I used to teach Sunday School, don't you want to see it?"

No, we didn't much, but out of loyalty to our dear Mummy, added to the fact that we were used to doing as we were told, we went, or rather were taken as we would not have been allowed to walk that distance by ourselves. As some solace, I went telling myself, "I hope I get a teacher who is young and pretty and wearing a nice hat!"

The only things I remember were the songs sung when we marched around during the collection, the chorus of which echoed pretty much the verse:

Dropping, dropping, dropping, dropping, hear the pennies fall,
Every one for Jesus, He shall have them all."

The other song was the goodbye one where, standing in a circle, we sang:

Teacher: Goodbye, goodbye, be always kind and true.
Children: Goodbye, goodbye, we will be kind and true!
Accompanied by much waving of little hands.

Early Holidays

I don't remember the first holiday to Sydney in 1934, at Aunty Stella and Uncle Bob's home at 32 Baxter Ave, Kogarah. My fifth birthday was celebrated there and, according to my Mother, the cake wasn't what I was anticipating and I must have shown it, so Uncle Bob told me: "this is a Sydney cake," and I accepted that. We had a trip to Taronga Zoo, and there must have been some thought that we might have a ride on the elephants, but Aunty Stella said "No" because she thought we might get fleas from

9

them! I have a postcard of a monkey riding a bicycle as a memento of that day.

We also went to Brighton-le-Sands to see the sea and I guess we saw it, but judging by the photos we didn't experience it. Dressed in our everyday clothes, rag hats pulled down low, dresses tucked into voluminous bloomers and with a little wave coming up behind us; we are still wearing our shoes and socks!

With Uncle Harry at Brighton-Le-Sands.

Holiday no.2 was a camping holiday at Stanwell Park, Wollongong, in 1937 or '38 with Aunty Pearl and Uncle Frank Gray and our cousins, Edith, Joyce and Betty, and Grandma Pereira. Grandma was a member of the Southwell tribe, with oodles of relations in the Dalton, Gunning and Goulburn areas, and on the way we stayed overnight on a farm with one of her cousins. Beds were made up on floors and we felt as though our adventure had begun.

Off again in the morning and, arriving at our destination, the business of setting up camp was new to us all, I believe. This time we really did get wet and did a bit of holding Dad's hand and jumping little waves. I don't believe any of our adults or children could swim, so we stayed safe and made sand castles mostly. With my complexion too much sun was not a good idea and we didn't have sunscreen then.

What I really remember were the ice creams obtainable at the kiosk close by; delicious big ones of colours and flavours we had never seen or tasted before. We had one each day and for a child of the Depression that was a big, big treat indeed. Elaine was most impressed by the fact that we were given the money to buy them ourselves!

Letters to Santa

The lack of money in the Depression for anything but absolute necessities showed through in one of my letters to Santa Claus.

In a very chatty letter written in 1937, in which I mentioned the temperature that day had been 110 at the Grenfell Post Office, and wished Santa a merry Christmas and not too busy a time, I just rather casually mentioned I would like a stroller or a lovely pram or any nice thing. Next year I wrote; *"I would like a humming top, or a rocking horse, or a car or something to ride about in, or a stroller. I guess these will be too dear so if you have not got them don't worry, but just give me anything you choose."* I did have a humming top among my toys so perhaps that was what Santa chose to give me that year. Needless to say I didn't ever get a rocking horse, or "something to ride about in" and is it any wonder when you realise I was within six weeks of my tenth birthday.

I went on to say *"There is a lot I would like to know about you and the fairies. I think you are connected with them."* Don't dare murmur something about the "sweet innocence of children"; to me it sounds like arrested development! A stroller did arrive some time later but I think I had Aunty Stella to thank for that.

Dear Aunty Mavis

Dear Aunty Mavis, the aunt every child would love to have, always patient and reassuring, full of love, and her lap, of generous proportions, was surely the most comfortable seat in the world.

My beloved Aunty Mavis.

Most Sunday afternoons when Elaine and I were little we would all go up to Spring Vale after church, often stay a while after tea, and a sleepy little girl called Beryl happily curled up on her

Aunty Mavis' lap, would say "Smooge?" and settle back to enjoy the touch of her aunt's fingers caressing her face, her hair. Bliss!

Aunty Mavis had several specialities when it came to cooking, including sausage rolls with tasty homemade filling and wonderfully light pastry. These were often a Mother's Day treat for the evening meal. Her scones won first prize at the Grenfell Show. 'Lilies' were another special treat: spoonfuls of sponge were cooked and wrapped around the handle of a wooden spoon while still warm in the shape of an Arum Lily flower. Later whipped cream was inserted in the "cup" part and a strip of firm yellow jelly placed to resemble the spadix. They were lovely for a "special" afternoon tea, but what a lot of time and fiddling around for something that would disappear in moments.

Big sultana cakes richly flavoured, with homemade butter and lunch cakes—very much like Welsh Cakes—were the staple fare for everyday afternoon teas, and lunches at shearing time.

At Christmas time Aunty Mavis used to make the sweets until the family grew quite big and my Grandfather George Henley Pereira (also known as G.H.P) forbade it as making too much work for her; which it was, especially in the heat standing over a hot stove. She used to make very special fondant based sweets and French jellies, plus others whose names I don't remember.

I now have the recipe book and the confectionary thermometer she used; I am almost reluctant to admit I haven't yet used either, perhaps it isn't too late? I do make yummy coconut ice but the recipe I use does not require a thermometer.

She was the mainstay of the family, often singing as she worked, a life cheerfully given for others. Her sister Eva married in April 1948, and Mavis became the sole carer for her mother, who died suddenly in December 1948, and her father, who died in January 1955.

Some time after that she moved to Young where her sister Ruby and husband Claude Wales lived, and had the new experience of living in her own home and being addressed as Miss Pereira. Uncle Claude died suddenly of a heart attack on 16th February 1970, and Aunty Ruby sold her house and came to live with Mavis.

One other memory: sometimes when nieces and nephews were making constant demands and she had just sat down for a break, Aunty Mavis would say "I can't come now, I've got a bone in my leg". And there was no arguing with that!

Aunty Mavis sometimes smilingly referred to herself as "an unclaimed treasure" and it was true of her and many other women of a similar age, with so many of our young men's lives being lost in World War One.

Ruby and Mavis lived very happily together until Mavis went to her well-earned reward on 24th July 1983. Aunty Ruby passed away on 8th April, 1985.

★★★★

There was always a cat: Barney

Barney, was just what I needed, the best friend, and we were so compatible. A gift from Aunty Pearl and Uncle Frank Gray at Christmas in 1939, he was a beautiful silver-grey half-Persian who didn't have really long fur—but it was thick and almost woolly.

He loved my doll's pram so I had the pleasure of wheeling him around in it, complete with comfortable mattress and pillow of course. Once I took him in the pram over to visit our next door neighbour, Mrs Thompson, probably half a mile away on a dirt road—the Mid-Western Highway. Actually, he thought it quite a normal thing to do.

He had unusual food tastes; he loved eating apricots and grapes, but never helped himself or was given them in his dish. The pair of us would climb up a branch of a big apricot tree where we could be seated comfortably and feast on apricots. I would break open the fruit, take small pieces and he would pull my hand with his paws to his mouth. Grapes were equally enjoyed, but down on terra firma.

Elaine, Barney, Peter and I.

While appreciating the fruit of the vine and orchard, Barney did not leave it all to us to supply his food. He was a very diligent hunter of mice, often rousing me at night with the little chirruping sounds he made after a catching a mouse, which meant he wanted me to go outside and praise him for his efforts. One time I especially remember; I went out to find five mice all in a tidy row, side by side, heads one end and tails the other, one for Dad, one for Mum, one for Elaine, one for me and one for himself. He could COUNT!

I left him at Cumnock Farm when I married on 3rd October, 1953. I have a letter I received from my mother telling me of his death in his sleep, in his 15th year. In the letter dated Sunday 28th February, 1954, my mother wrote *"Well my pet, I have got to tell you, our dear Barney is dead. He was just as usual, only a little slower and Dad found him Thursday afternoon, just dead in his sleep. It made us all sad, but we have got to be thankful he did not suffer and we are lucky to have such a dear pet for 14 years and 2 months. Now don't you fret too much, he was happy to the end, I was talking to him that morning and saw him lying asleep in the shade of the house and he never moved."*

Jimmy was also given to us by Aunty Pearl and Uncle Frank Gray. He was a half-brother to Barney and I think about two years younger. Jimmy was personality plus and won the hearts of everyone. He had deep gold markings, almost auburn. He too had an unusual taste in food, not apricots and grapes but almonds. Sadly we didn't have him long enough, perhaps two years; he was bitten by a snake and died a painful death. We all grieved deeply for dear little Jimmy.

★★★★

Our Home: Merrilea

Our home was called 'Merrilea', although it has since been renamed as Bungalong. It is on the Bungalong Creek, 11 miles east of Grenfell on the Cowra Road. The home was made of rammed earth and brick walls with a corrugated iron roof and bull-nose verandahs facing south and west. It had six rooms.

The Kitchen

When visitors came to our place, they usually came to the back door, and on knocking would be welcomed into the kitchen. There was no hallway in the house and the door opened straight into the kitchen which was the centre room at the back of the house. The floor was covered with linoleum which, according to the custom of the times, was washed and polished each week. I still remember well the feel and smell of spreading the wax on the floor with a pad made of old sheeting and the energy needed by me, down on my hands and knees, to rub it off with vim and vigour, to obtain a good shine. The bedrooms and dining room also had linoleum, the other rooms had bare boards.

The kitchen table was where everything happened: where the meals were prepared and eaten, cakes made, fruit from our orchard prepared for making jam, sauces and preserves, butter was made from the cream that came from the separator, and the ironing done on several layers of blanket covered by sheeting.

With Mum and Elaine,
enjoying home-grown watermelon.

Getting ready to make melon jam provided more opportunities for diversion and entertainment than any other fruit. Dad always had the job of peeling and cutting up the melon into slices. Then Elaine and I did our bit, getting the seeds out. They were extremely slippery so it was very easy to flip them at each other and perhaps even at our parents, 'accidently on purpose', as we used to say. With lemon, orange, ginger or pineapple added, it made a very enjoyable jam.

The Christmas pudding too, was concocted at the kitchen table, with everyone having a stir for luck. We didn't eat it at Christmas as my mother was very aware of her Scottish—McKensie—side of her ancestry. I remember her saying that the Scotch made more of New Year and saw Christmas as a Popish celebration, so we had our pudding at New Year. That said, we always spent Christmas day at Spring Vale, and helped to eat their pudding.

There was no sink or running water so the washing up was done on the kitchen table; washed in a tin dish and drained on a really big tray. The drying up was often done by mother's little helpers. Hot water came from a large kettle on top of the stove, which was lit first thing in the morning and kept alight all day. The washing-up water was carried outside and thrown on the garden. In the early days one had to go outside to a tap near the back door and that was where the men washed their hands after work before coming inside. I can just remember when Dad piped the water inside to a tap just inside the back door with a bucket under to catch the drips. Hardly luxury, but at least it saved steps and going outside in the cold weather.

We still have the original kitchen chairs, one in the *en suite*, one in my husband George's office and two, which were painted cream at some time, in the guest room. The dresser is now in our lounge room with the dinner set that was a wedding present from my sister displayed on its shelves alongside other interesting pieces, including a cheese dish and my very special one piece of Clarice Cliff, which was a wedding present from Aunty Ruby and Uncle Claude, and has a waterlily design.

The only other pieces of furniture were a two-tiered cupboard made by Dad to hold cooking utensils—now at Cumnock Farm, where my son Murray and his wife Marian live, in what was previously the laundry—and a stool also made by Dad to go along the wall next to the kitchen table for Elaine and I to sit on. I used to sit on my legs, was corrected for doing it, but continued to do so. The stool is now on our back verandah, traces of green paint still visible on its sides, and the top is well-polished by our bottoms sliding along it. The fireplace, with its large wood-burning stove, occupied most of one wall with the mantel shelf above it covered with a green oilskin valance scalloped for decorative effect. On the shelf was a set of canisters decorated with pictures of views of Sydney Harbour. On the wall behind was a framed copy of a calendar picture of a little girl sitting up in bed, breakfast in front, a very interested dog on one side and a hopeful cat on the other. It was always there and is now on our dining room wall, looking down on our table.

The Back Room

The room to the right of the kitchen was called the "Back Room" and it had a bit of everything in it. The telephone was on the back wall just inside the door from the kitchen. We were on a party line with a lot of other people so you had to listen for your own ring and resist the temptation to listen in to others' conversations, being aware that maybe someone else was listening to yours. To make a call you would wind the handle in "shorts" and "longs" to correspond with morse code. Our number was 186V—dit, dit, dit, dah, or short, short, short, long.

A window was opposite the door—did it have hinges on one side and open out *into* the room? I believe it did. How strange! A three-quarter bed stood beside the wall; Elaine and I used to move out there sometimes when we had guests and give them our room. Sometimes there were more than two guests and I now wonder just where we fitted them in. We did have some folding camp beds dating from our first camping holiday at Stanwell Park near Wollongong. Perhaps in summer they would be placed on the front verandah where the thick Virginia Creeper vine provided some shelter.

Back to the "back room". Above the bed and the full length of the room was where the outdoor hats and coats were hung. Against the opposite wall was a small table. Mum's Singer sewing machine and Dad's shaving stand shared the space, and around the corner was a linen cupboard, yes, made by Dad. A big box under the window contained among other things some of our baby clothes, shoes and shawls, and we loved looking at them.

Dad also had his guns and rifles stashed away in a corner. Goodness knows what else may have been there or what it may have been used for. Dad had been doing something there one time which involved galvanised iron. I somehow managed to cut my left knee on a sharp edge when I was about six or seven-years-old, so it was off to hospital where Dr. Fenwick said "Ginger for pluck" and proceeded to stitch it up without any injections or painkillers. It was quite a large cut and when the stitches were taken out it all fell apart and the scar remains to this day, 75 years later.

The Storeroom

Originally it was just that, a storeroom, but as Elaine and I grew bigger Dad procured some timber and built a bathroom into the corner nearest the kitchen. He installed a bath and chip heater, connected water, added a washstand and a butter box for something to sit on and there we were. Opposite was a cupboard that held saucepans, shoe cleaning polish and brushes, big kitchen utensils, as well as the cream separator when it was not being used.

Around the walls were a sugar box, a big flour bin, two lots of shelving for jams and preserves—visitors were frequently taken to admire the rows of jams and bottles of beautifully packed fruit as part of the entertainment—a cool safe, a tin of kerosene for filling lamps; and at one time an incubator with chickens hatching in it!

More or less in the middle of the area was an upright log which was the separator stand. I used to take turns at doing the separating, turning the handle at the right pace—sixty turns a minute—and watching the cream flow into a bowl placed on a special stand and the skim milk into a bucket below. A big wash up followed, as everything needed to be scalded with boiling water after the initial wash. I also learned to make the butter from the cream and still have one of the grooved bats that were used to shape the pats of butter. My mother used to like the buttermilk for making scones.

There was no "WC" of course; one took a walk 'down the back' where the 'little house' could be seen sheltered by a white lucerne tree and a Honey Bush (*Melianthus major*). Although I didn't know its name for a long time, I had always been interested in the bush with its unusually shaped and coloured leaves and striking dark plum flowers. A friend, Lorna Flanagan, gave us a plant of it years ago when we lived out at Cumnock Farm. About seven years ago, when visiting the farm, I saw a piece broken off. I brought it home, popped it in a pot and thankfully it grew and is a prominent feature in our front garden. When in Tasmania in 2006 we visited Port Arthur and were very interested to see it used extensively in their garden planted with plants that would have been grown in the convict days.

Our Parents' Bedroom

In our parents' bedroom there was a rather lovely metal bed with a white Marcella quilt, and sometimes pillow shams with crochet lace edging and insertion which would have been made by my great grandmother, Nana Foulkes.

The bedroom suite consisted of an oak wardrobe and dressing table, which were later given to our youngest daughter, Jeanette, for a 21st birthday gift. The third piece was the washstand with lovely deep rose tiles at the back, which is now in our guest room, the original jug and basin set on its marble top. The basin has been used in different ways; there is a photo of baby Elaine in it, so it was probably where she was bathed until she grew too big. It has also been used for mixing Christmas puddings and fruit cakes that were too large for other available bowls, including the two-tiered wedding cake I made for Jeanette and Simon, who were married on 4th October, 1986. Behind the door was Mum's old tin trunk containing some of her treasures.

Other furnishings included a lowboy for Dad's clothes, a padded butter box for Dad to sit on whilst pulling on his boots, and the cot, also made by Dad, with its lovely Marcella quilt on it too. The final touch was a lovely picture of a little boy leaning out of a window to reach a bird, and a beautiful angel beside guarding him. It is now in our guest room.

Our Bedroom

Elaine and I always shared a bedroom, quite amiably. Our two single iron beds covered with white counterpanes were each against a wall; between us under the window was a piece of "bush furniture". This was constructed from kerosene boxes padded and covered with cretonne fabric, curtains at front and providing a seat in the middle and some storage below, the two sides being higher to give more storage for shoes, books and so on. The oak wardrobe was so narrow that coat hangers had to be slanted to fit. The matching small dressing table had a scorch mark near the bottom right of the mirror where a candle had been placed too close to it.

Later, another wardrobe was bought; this one having a lovely waratah motif carved either side of the bevelled glass mirror. It is now in our guest room. There was also room for a big chest of drawers, now in our second guest room. It would be interesting to see this with the coats of paint removed and appropriate handles added.

I don't think we could have enjoyed the pleasure of reading in bed at night very much as electricity didn't come to our area until 1950 or 1951, not long before we moved, as Dad had bought Cumnock Farm. Our lighting was a candle or kerosene lamp on the dressing table at the foot of my bed.

The Front Room

Entering through the front door, which was in the centre of the south wall facing the Mid-Western Highway, one entered a large dining room sometimes referred to as the "Front Room". A large oak dining table stood in the centre of the room and this was always covered by a table cloth. There were two oak carvers, as they were called, and six oak dining chairs. An oak sideboard was against the eastern wall and it is in this room (our dining room) as I write. The same objects are still on it as then, namely: a jardinière, an angel that was given to my mother when she was a girl, two ruby glass pieces—a jug and a little bowl on a silver stand, a biscuit barrel and two large shells. The angel was made in Germany in Victorian times and is Biscuit-ware.

Also on that wall was Mum's old Estey Organ which now stands in our hallway with one of her Carnival glass bowls in pride of place, alongside some of our own collectables. My mother's father, Walter King brought the organ from Temora in a spring cart not long after she and Alf were married on 6th June, 1923. Until a piano was bought some years later, the organ was the main musical instrument in the house apart from Dad's violin and Hawaiian steel guitar. Between these furnishings was the door into the bedroom I shared with my sister Elaine.

At the other end of the room, a big open fireplace with mantel protruded into the room, alongside the door into our parent's bedroom. A lovely rug was in front, and on the right side were my father's easy chair and the wireless in the recess. On the left side was my mother's rocking chair, and behind it a bookcase that Dad had built from the piano case. The piano was bought in about 1940.

Both the rocking chair and the bookcase are now in our daughter Kathy's home in East St. Grenfell. Other furnishings were a chaise lounge which was passed down from Spring Vale, a gramophone that sat on a cupboard with records in it, and an old wireless cabinet made into a music cabinet. Lighting was provided by a kerosene Miller lamp. Pictures on the wall included a lovely pair now in our lounge room: *Williams Creek near Newcastle* and *Harbour View near Folly Point*. I love them.

Our lighting was candles, as well as Miller and Aladdin lamps that each used kerosene for fuel. However, my Dad was a very inventive handyman and wired our house for electricity, which was supplied by a wind-powered generator. While we weren't able to use it all the time, it was very convenient to have it to turn on when we came home late at night, or when going into a dark room if nothing more.

The Rocking Chair

There is an amusing tale to tell about the rocking chair, which was the 1923 Christmas present from the Spring Vale family to my mother, Grace. Alf's sisters, Mavis and Ruby, were given the responsibility of driving the horse and sulky to Grenfell, buying the chair and bringing it home.

Apparently there was a threat of rain because, after they arrived home and the chair was safely hidden from view, Aunty Ruby was heard to say in Mum's hearing, "we would have made a pretty picture driving along with a rocking chair held over our heads". There was dismay among those there as they wondered whether Grace had heard. Was the surprise spoilt? Grace had heard but it hadn't registered as being anything to do with her, so there was still a lovely surprise awaiting her on Christmas Day.

The chair, with wooden rockers, cane frame, made from seagrass, and with a diamond pattern woven into the centre back, has continued to have a life over four generations of our family. Baby Elaine was photographed in it, as was our daughter Kathy and, later, her daughter Linda.

My sister Elaine in the rocking chair,
December 1926.

I remember my Mother being seated in it at one side of the fireplace, the bookcase behind, my Dad on the other side, perhaps working away on one of the wool mats that he made (some of which we still have), both listening to 'The Village Glee Club'. Elaine and I would be seated at the table doing our homework by the light of the Miller kerosene lamp.

There was another member of the family who appreciated the chair too, especially if it had a soft cushion or two in it. That was our beloved bluey-grey cat, Barney, and if an unthinking visitor took possession of it, he would plant himself in front of that person and glare in a manner that was hard to mistake: "Get out of my chair"!

I think it is time to visit my daughter, Kathy, who is the present custodian of the chair, and spend … some …. time …. gently….

.… rocking.

Saturday preparation for Sunday

We didn't have a bathroom for a number of years. We bathed in a big round galvanised iron tub in front of the kitchen fire in winter at least; and probably throughout the year, as it was handy to the hot and cold water. Saturday night was bath night of course, and the routine was youngest first and so on, Dad last. Our hair was also washed, dried a little and then we were seated on a low box while Mum put our hair in "rags".

Our hair was styled in sausage curls from early childhood until our mid-teens. Pictured in 1934.

This involved having strips of old sheeting torn a little over an inch wide; we held one end firmly while the other went over our head and Mum parted our hair and twirled it around her end of the "rag", starting about ear level I think, and moving downwards, then wrapping it in our part of the rag and tying a knot to keep everything in place, then working her way around the head until all was done. The next day the rags were unwrapped, and there we were, with sausage curls as many photos will testify. I'm sure we were the only girls for miles around who wore their hair like that when in their teens!

There were all sorts of hazards when it came to ladies' hairdressing it seems. I quote from a letter written by me to my mother when she was in hospital at Young at the end of 1944:

"I washed my hair and Daddy put it in rags, and was terribly pleased with himself. I combed all the knots out of it first, and you should have seen it all brushed out. Daddy made a fairly good job of it, but forgot to curl the ends so they stayed straight at the end, and the curls went something like this 00—. Also instead of parting the top part into two, downwards like this |, he parted it across, like this—. Still, it looks O.K. today. (Monday)"

Our lives followed a regular, simple pattern. On Saturday, Mum would cook whichever joint of mutton it was our turn to have, leg or ribs, ready for our Sunday lunch. She also cleaned Dad's shoes. No work was done on Sunday except what was necessary for the animals. Dad worked very hard all the week and would have welcomed a 'sleep in' and 'Sabbath Rest'. 2pm found us in our places in the Cowra Road Methodist Church as it was then, dressed in our Sunday best. My Dad was sometimes organist if his sister Eva was away. When Aunty Eva married in 1948 I became the organist. Church was followed by Sunday School. Those who weren't teachers spent the time outside standing in little groups or sitting in cars catching up on the news.

The Pereira sisters did all the cleaning of the church, and brought and arranged the flowers each week. My grandparents George and Charlotte Pereira were married there on 20th March, 1895 and also my parents on 6th June, 1923.

Sunday School Picnics

These were annual events held about the same time as the Sunday School Anniversary, in the spring, always at Spring Vale on a flat beyond the farm buildings where a skillion on one shed could be used for the tables of food, shelter and prizes for races. The usual games were played in the morning: twos and threes, drop the handkerchief and perhaps rounders; whatever people chose to organise. At a certain age I would be hoping I could find a lady who would let me wheel her baby around in its pram. When lunch time came I was always on the lookout for a cake with caramel icing, something I loved.

I recall the first time I tasted baked beans was in a sandwich at a Sunday School picnic, and I thought it was delicious. That reminds me of a joke Dad told and chuckled over: "Two blokes sit down at lunch time. Opening up their boxes; the first chap says: 'Jam sandwiches again, I hate jam sandwiches.' His mate says: 'Why don't you tell your missus you hate them?' First chap: 'My missus is away on holiday and I'm making my own sandwiches'."

Races were in the afternoon, arranged according to age and sex. I can't recall ever winning but didn't disgrace myself. Elaine was always among the last.

Other amusements during the afternoon were stepping the distance, balls in the bucket, three-legged races, and thread the needle. Winners were rewarded with prizes.

There were races for ladies and gents too, of course, and the rewards for these were conversation lollies. There is still one here which Dad gave to Mum, perhaps in 1923 or '24 with the words *I need you* imprinted on it. It is safely boxed in Mum's old tin trunk with some of her other treasures including her wedding veil.

In the evening, a concert was always held and from earliest memories I enjoyed them greatly as there was so much ready

29

participation. Mum's Journal says for 16th October 1942: *The Sunday School Picnic was held and at night the concert held in S.V.'s dining room.* According to Mum's journal I played my first piano solo for the public, and Peter Diprose and I sang a duet, *No Sir, No Sir:*

> He: *Tell me one thing, tell me truly, Tell me why you scorn me so,*
> *Tell me why, when asked a question, You will always answer, no.*
> She: *No sir, No sir. No, Sir, No.*

> She: *My father was a Spanish Captain, And before he went to sea*
> *He told me to be sure and answer 'No' to all you said to me.*
> *No sir, No sir, No sir, No!*

> He: *If when walking in the garden, Picking flowers all wet with dew,*
> *Tell me, would you be offended, If I walked and talked with you?*
> She: *No sir, No sir, No sir, No.*

> He: *If, when walking in the garden I should ask you to be Mine*
> *And should tell you that I love you, Would you then my heart decline?*
> She: *Oh no sir, No sir, No sir, No!*

Doing our bit for the Sunday School concert:
Margaret Hughes, Elaine and I (right to left).

Once a year the Sunday School Anniversary was held. This
was the one and only time each year that Elaine and I had a new
dress. The children received a book prize and contributed some
special singing for which they had been practising, diligently
trained by my Dad. Once again I refer to Mum's Journal, 11th
October 1942: "*Sunday School Anniversary. Elaine and Beryl sang alto
in two pieces, 'Smile and Be Cheerful' and 'Happiness is in the Air'.*"

P.S. Many years later I trained and played piano for a junior
choir (robed) in our church in Grenfell and, in a book I kept,
noted we sang *Smile and Be Cheerful* on 1st March 1970, 17
children present.

Harvest Thanksgiving

This was always a joyous, meaningful celebration to those
who worshipped at Cowra Road Methodist Church. All were

farming folk who produced a lot of what they ate and needed the money from the sale of wool and wheat to pay for all the other things required.

On the Saturday afternoon, Elaine and I would accompany Dad on a trip to the Chinese market gardeners who would give us some of their produce to add to the display. Their garden was on the left bank of the Brundah Creek, before crossing on the road to Brundah Falls. I always kept pretty close to Dad while there and we didn't go inside the building they had, but some very alien smells seemed to come forth from it.

Then in the evening people would come to the church with their offerings, choosing their best of course. In front of the pulpit, tables were set up in tiers to display the fruits to their best advantage; perhaps sheaves of wheat at the sides, bigger things like pumpkins and watermelons on the floor. When we were really little, Elaine and I would be given a piece of cloth to help by polishing apples so they would look lovely and shiny. Then all was arranged, grapes prominent, and a loaf of bread and jug of water were placed in the centre as symbols of our basic needs.

A Harvest Thanksgiving,
similar to those of my childhood.

On Sunday at 2pm and again at night, as we entered the church we were greeted by the combined aromas of grain, vegetables, fruit and flowers:

[Pause, take a deep breath and breathe it in!]

And didn't we lift up our voices and *sing*, led by my grandmother Charlotte and Aunty Mavis, who both possessed lovely clear voices.

The hymns in the Harvest section of the Methodist Hymn Book were wonderful, for example, No. 962:

> *Come, ye thankful people, come, Raise the song of harvest home:*
> *All is safely gathered in, Ere the winter storms begin;*
> *God our Maker doth provide For our wants to be supplied:*
> *Come to God's own temple, come, Raise the song of harvest home.'*

No. 967—

> *Now the year is crowned with blessing As we gather in the grain;*
> *And, our grateful thanks expressing, Loud we raise a joyous strain,*
> *Bygone days of toil and sadness Cannot now our peace destroy;*
> *For the hills are clothed with gladness, And the valleys shout with joy.*

> **To the Lord their first fruits bringing**
> **All His thankful people come**
> **To the Father praises singing For the joy of harvest home.**

No. 963—
We plough the fields, and scatter The good seed on the land,
But it is fed and watered By God's almighty hand;
He sends the snow in winter, The warmth to swell the grain,
The breezes and the sunshine, And soft refreshing rain.

All good gifts around us Are sent from heaven above;
Then thank the Lord, O thank the Lord, For all His love.

I wish you could have been there to hear that, sung from the heart.

Another memory of the Chinese gardeners was the weekly appearance of their horse-drawn dray loaded with vegetables grown on their garden and covered with damp hessian to keep them fresh. We knew when to look out for them. Elaine and I would go to the roadside with Mum and watch with interest to see what they had and what Mum would buy.

The Show

The annual Grenfell Pastoral, Agricultural, and Horticultural Show was an event looked forward to with much anticipation. First stop for us was usually the Pavilion to look at entries there, then off down Sideshow Alley where the calls of spruikers and the beat of the big drum, combined with rapid ding dong of the bell up on the stage of Jimmy Sharman's boxing tent, really revved up the excitement. The boxers stood up there, wearing silk dressing gowns over the boxing shorts, ready to take on local contenders who were looking for a few minutes of glory. We rarely went inside any of the sideshows but there was always plenty of entertainment going on outside and I think we always had a ride on the merry-go-round. The show was often a get-together of families and as lunch time approached they would assemble, spread rugs on the ground between parked cars and enjoy a meal and time together. Judging from the one photo I have, some ladies and children donned aprons! Good idea.

Lunch at the Show in the early 1930's. Several of the ladies and children can be seen wearing aprons.

The year 1941 was a remarkable one. My Mother won first prize for half a dozen Gem Scones, the trophy being a silver tray in a padded blue satin box that is now in my sideboard. It wasn't remarkable that Mum should win; she made very good gem scones. What was remarkable was that *I* made and entered a sponge roll in the twelve-and-under class and it too won FIRST prize. It was probably the very best sponge roll I ever made so after that I rested on my laurels. That is, until I made some apple jelly in 1976 and gave a jar to Mum to eat. Instead she entered it in the show and it won. I'm sure she ate it later.

My parents became enthusiastic supporters of the Grenfell Show, particularly in the '70s and early '80s when their Dagmar Street garden and orchard had become established and productive.

My Mother had joined the Country Women's Association years previously, but had been unable to attend meetings until they came to town to live. She then grasped the opportunity to learn a number of different crafts with both hands—literally—and became very skilful with them and gained much enjoyment. She also entered some of her handiwork in the Show.

Aunty Dot was widowed in 1967, but each year one of the family would drive to Temora and bring her back to Grenfell for several weeks around Show time. She was a keen and excellent knitter, so she and Mum would pore over the schedule and see what entries she could find for the open section and also what Mum and Dad had which they could enter.

Each year followed the same pattern; they would buy some ham off the bone, make sandwiches and Mum would fill a Thermos with her superlative coffee which was made with freshly ground coffee from her little hand grinder plus a tiny pinch of salt. With those and some of Aunty Dot's delicious slices they enjoyed a picnic lunch after going to the pavilion to see how successful their entries had been.

Later in the afternoon they would meet some friends and sit ringside and enjoy the ring events. This pattern continued until they were into their eighties. Mum continued to exhibit after Dad had passed away.

In 1981 when Dad was eighty-two and Mum eighty-four, they won the following prizes:

Mum: 1st—for three citrus jams and the Kath Smith Trophy
      1st—Lemon jam   1st—Quince jelly
      1st—3 Stock blooms
      1st—Jonquils   2nd—Grapefruit jam
      2nd—Nectarine jam
      2nd—3 Daffodils—non trumpet.
Dad   1st—Rhubarb   1st—Eschallots.
Mum 1st—Handicraft not mentioned. This was a celluloid shopping basket to which the judge gave full marks—10 out of 10—and said it was very well done with no mistakes. To me this was amazing because Mum had very poor eyesight.

Dust Coats

In some old photographs you will note the men, and sometimes the ladies, wearing a garment that looks like a light-coloured elongated shirt or coat. They were known as dust coats, necessary sometimes to protect the clothes underneath from dust that blew up from dirt roads when other cars met or passed. The cars themselves didn't keep much dust out despite side curtains made of canvas with celluloid windows, which could be clipped on and off.

My grandparents George and Charlotte with baby
Elaine. Pa is wearing the dust coat that was often a
necessity when travelling.

Aprons and the Pereiras

Judging by family photographs covering 60 years, aprons were
an important part of the wardrobe. How versatile they were; apart
from the obvious use of protecting what was underneath when
one was cooking, doing housework and so on.

We had a large orchard, and when fruit was ripening we
would go around each day, pick some and place it in a bucket.
If there were windfalls on the ground, one gathered up the hem
and corners of the apron to make a bag and the fallen fruit was
placed in there.

The same thing happened if one came unexpectedly across
a nest of eggs laid by a hen who thought she had found a lovely

hidden place to lay her eggs. Once again the apron was converted into a receptacle to carry them home to be tested for freshness by placing in a bowl of water to see if any floated.

The aprons made their appearance in many photos of earlier generations at most unexpected times, one being the gathering of the clan for a picnic lunch at the Show at Grenfell in the very early thirties. Another photo was taken on the back verandah of Aunty Betty and Uncle Arthur's home, probably not long after they were married. Aunty Betty's parents were in the photo, also some of her relations, and evidently Aunties Mavis and Eva and Grandma had been invited to come and meet them and there they were, all in their aprons.

My grandma Charlotte, mother Grace and aunts Mavis
and Eva wore aprons as part of their daily attire.

I sometimes wondered whether my mother felt not completely dressed unless she was wearing an apron. Often, when asked for a visit to our place, she would arrive wearing her apron and I would say, "Mum, I didn't ask you out here for you to work!" And her reply would be, "I might be able to do something to help."

Her one requirement of an apron was that it should have a pocket for her handkerchief (I can relate to that). If she had been given an apron without the required essential pocket, she would search in a box which held remnants of materials and find a piece; it did not matter how alien. She once chose a nursery design, with teddy bears. In no time it would have been cut out, sewn on and Mum had her pocket!

In 1984, while in Titisee in Germany's Black Forest, I saw an attractive apron on display, thought it would be a suitable gift to take home for Mum, so I bought it. The material was blue and white striped cotton decorated with much lace, embroidery and frills. I'm afraid I didn't think at the time how time consuming the task of ironing it would be but it did have TWO POCKETS!

Mum's Journal: 25th March 1943— Mrs Bridger, Granddaughter of Con O'Brien

"Sunday we had a nice service when a beautiful communion table was given by Mrs Ida Bridger in memory of her Grandfather the late Con O'Brien who was a member of the church in the early days back as far as seventy years ago, he was the first man to discover gold in the district and was also a loyal Methodist. Mrs Bridger also gave a cushion cover in memory of her Mother. These beautiful gifts were thankfully received by the trustees. Mr Sam Starr presented the table and Mrs G Pereira the cushion cover on Mrs Bridger's behalf as she was unable to be present."

16th April 1943—Pa and Grandma, Mavis and Eva and Mrs Bridger were down to see us on Sunday. Mrs Bridger gave a photo of her grandfather to the citizens of Grenfell, and we saw it presented and hung in the Council chambers on Saturday morning 15th April. We had the opportunity to see Mrs Bridger several times as she stayed at Spring Vale. She lived at Petersham and was a piano teacher. She became interested in Elaine and I, and gave us three music books all signed by her, *The Old Refrain*, an album of popular songs—specifically for *When it's Lamp Lighting Time in the Valley*, and a copy of *Variations on Home Sweet Home* for Elaine. By the look of the latter I don't think Elaine ever learned it; I certainly do not remember hearing it. Our teacher Miss Procter would never have given us anything like it for our study! That aside, we had some good musical evenings together and I particularly remember one time when we were up at Spring Vale, there was a storm outside and inside Mrs Bridger was playing *The Storm*, a very dramatic descriptive composition. She was amazing; it was hard to decide just where some of the sound was coming from, it mingled so incredibly.

We have a photo of Mr Bridger with Elaine and I and our three pet lambs, and Mrs Bridger's autographs in our Autograph books.

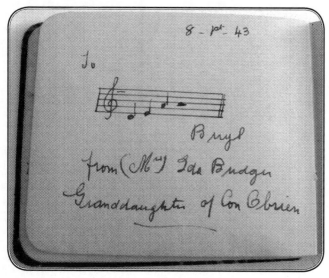

My Autograph book.

****

There was always a cat: Timmie

On Friday, 6th November 1953, my husband George and I visited Aunty Pearl and Uncle Frank and our cousins at Greenethorpe for tea and then attended a concert given by the Young Methodist Church. Soon after our arrival at 'Renown' they had shown us a little striped stray kitten snuggled up to a sick chook in their laundry and asked would we like to give him a home. Being the cat lovers we were we didn't hesitate. Yes, we wanted him! He grew into a very handsome cat with a lovely thick coat, a mix of black, fawn and tawny.

Timmie.

I used to write letters home to 'Cumnock Farm' in between visits, so will quote from a few of the early ones. There was usually some comment about Timmie even if only that George had shot a couple of rabbits for his enjoyment.

19 November 1953: "*Young Timmie is as good as a circus and growing so fast that you would hardly know him. He is very playful and one of his favourite games is for him to get inside the legs of a chair; lean over a rung, and then we box each other. He is going to dish up all the cats in Watta when he is a big boy, so we say. He is great company and we are both fond of him. If he accidently gets hurt or trodden on—he doesn't give one great yowl but cries and whimpers softly for a couple of minutes and it is enough to melt a heart of stone.*"

Wednesday 2 December: "*Mary came over this afternoon with a jug of iced orange drink for me and brought her little yellow kitten and he and Timmie had a happy game together, then both fell asleep after their excitement.*"

In mid-December we went to the furniture sale of Rev. Rowe of the Anglican Church at Grenfell and bought a cane chair and a sideboard. In a letter to Mum dated 19 December I wrote: "*Timmie thinks our best buy was the easy chair, he tried it out before it had been in the house five minutes and pronounced it to be the very thing he had been needing. He is curled up on my lap at present purring his head off.*"

Monday, 1 February 1954: "*I have the dearest little kitten curled up asleep on my knee—golly, he is a darling, we just think him just right and are so proud of his beautiful tail.*"

Sunday, 28 May: "*Our kitten is as beautiful as ever. George weighed him on our kitchen scales a couple of nights ago and he is about nine pounds. It made a real picture; all our weights, four pounds of sugar, a tin of peaches and one of pilchards on one end of the scales and Timmie in the basket Grays gave us on the other; taking it all quite happily.*"

Dear Timothy the cat continued to be a valued part of our lives, giving much companionship and pleasure, accepting the changes that came.

In 1960, George bought some land near Cumnock Farm, sold his share of 'Pontefract Park' to his brother, Stan, and we moved to Grenfell approximately mid-June. We stayed the first week with Mum and Dad, then moved into the shearers hut with a borrowed caravan for our children Alison and David to sleep in. It was found to leak and not suitable for winter so they moved back with their grandparents.

I was pregnant with twins, very uncomfortable and not capable of doing much to look after my family, and just about living on raw Uncle Toby's Oats and spoonfuls of dry Sunshine powdered milk. Something had to be done so George and I went shopping for a house in town and chose 22—as it was then—Weddin Street, and moved in the first week in August.

Through all these upheavals Timmie stayed with us; we were his family and he trusted us and the children loved him too. Early 1965 we knew all was not well with him as he seemed in pain when we picked him up. The time had come to say farewell to our dear furry friend who had been part of our family for nearly 12 years.

★★★★

My Education

I commenced school at Brundah North Provisional, a one-teacher school, on the 31st October 1935 aged six years and eight months. The teacher was Victor Smith. Perhaps the idea of starting a few weeks before the Christmas holidays was to give me a taste of what was to come. By the time the next year commenced I was seven or within a few days of my birthday.

According to my Mother, I had already taught myself to read from the Bib and Bub Book she had made by cutting out and pasting the coloured May Gibbs comics on brown paper. Pa had saved these from a newspaper he bought and read. In later years my own children were able to enjoy listening to or reading these stories when they visited their grandparents. Now, 75 years later, these comics are a little worn from use, but still safe in my keeping.

So   *The Cat Sat on the rag mat.*
        The Cat Can see the rat.
        The Rat Can not see the Cat etc
did not pose any difficulty for me.

School with Cyril Fowler

I do not have many memories of my first year at school, but have the feeling that while it was tolerable, it was not inspiring. So it was well that Mr Smith left at the end of the year and Cyril Fowler was appointed in 1937. He was a cousin of my Grandfather, and a man very dedicated to his vocation. He was rather predictable in his choice of subjects for compositions; "A beautiful morning in spring", "One misty morning in winter", and similar—just pile the adjectives in and we were right. Another forte was memory training. We learned a lot of poetry and at the end of the term— there were three in a year then—we had to submit a list of 20 poems and be able to recite any he might choose. In one of Elaine's poetry books I have the list she prepared one of those years.

Music was another subject Mr Fowler spent time on. He could play the violin and sometimes brought it along to help teach us a song. If no violin was available a tuning fork was used to give us the starting note. It was struck on the desk, the point quickly put down on the same and that was our starting note—DOH. We had to keep singing it, in varying degrees of accuracy, until we finally "got it". He also taught Elaine and I the alto for *Silent Night, O Holy Night* to sing at a Christmas break up, as well as the alto of *Oh, who will o'er the Downs with me*. I learned these so well that, more than seventy years later, if asked to sing that song I would launch into the alto, not soprano, although I know it too.

There was an open fireplace at the end the pupils faced and no shortage of wood around, so in winter we would have a fire to help keep us warm. I have pleasant memories of some people bringing milk, sugar, cocoa and presumably a saucepan, and of us being able to have a nice hot cup of cocoa at lunch times during one winter. It didn't become a habit or tradition, just a nice diversion while it lasted.

We all joined in most of the playtime activities; rounders, hide and seek, sometimes marbles, and other games from time to time. I remember a game we called Three Jolly Welshmen which had two teams who lined up at opposite ends of the playground. One team marched up to the other chanting "Three Jolly Welshmen looking for a job". The other responded, "Show us some of your handiwork", which was the signal for the first group to mime the actions associated with whatever job they had chosen. When guessed correctly they ran; those caught had to join the other team. I don't remember if it went on until all were caught or whether they swapped roles. The number of children attending varied over the years from 14 to 17.

If it rained in the morning Mr Fowler would come and take Elaine and I to school in his car. When told that, our cousin Edith Gray was scandalised and gasped, "Does he?" Didn't we poor things ever get a break from school?

Nature study was another subject; there were plenty of resources, lots of different leaves and creepy crawlies. One time we climbed over the back fence and went right up the hill behind, pushing our way through and around numerous Golden Orb spider webs and finally coming back with bunches of beautiful mauve mint bush (*Prostanthera*) that grew at the top. Nature study with a difference. That little excursion was in Mr Fowler's successor's time and I think our teacher was relieved when we reappeared.

Under Mr Fowler I progressed through second class and skipped third. My best subjects were English and Spelling and in the four years he was there I received awards at the end of the year for Spelling and General Proficiency. Sometime in those years my tonsils and adenoids were removed. I recall a very painful recovery.

Thanks to Mr Fowler we enjoyed a great experience in June 1940. While not rejoicing in the fact that my mother needed time in hospital at that time, I am glad to have two letters that we wrote to her. I will quote from Elaine's diary dated 7th June, 1940: *"Last night when we got home, Mr Fowler asked us would we like to see* Gulliver's Travels *and our darling Daddy said we could. Mr Fowler took Ernie, John, Connie, Teddy, Beryl and I, Aunty Mavis and Aunty Eva. He was pleased with himself and said he felt like a father!* Gulliver's Travels *was very nice, though not as nice as* Snow White *but Beryl and I fell in love with Gulliver's voice and looks. I liked the news very much—I saw Hitler and Chamberlain."*

After Mr Fowler left at the end of 1940 he would come back to visit from time to time, and in 1987 he gave Elaine and I each a copy of his book, *The Meanderings of a Bush Pedagogue.*

When Mr Fowler left, the Second World War had been going over a year. With an Army Camp at Cowra we sometimes had convoys passing by, occasionally overtaking us as we rode. My parents were going to first aid classes and learning camouflage-net making. With all this we were well aware of the war.

As I mentioned, we rode our bikes. Others who travelled the same direction but had further to go were Peter and Bruce Diprose, both younger than Elaine and I, and Bruce Brown on Trixie the horse. (Bruce married my cousin, Betty Gray, in 1957.)

North Brundah students, circa 1937
(I'm fifth from the left).

The highway was gravelled, often corrugated but kept in reasonable order by "The Grader Man", Mr Abbott I think. One day, coming home, Bruce's bike became caught up in a heap of the gravel as a car was overtaking us and over he went. The car stopped and two ladies came back to see how he was and brought some chocolate for him. I had often eyed those big slabs of chocolate in a glass case at Purdies; as you could buy it then by weight, unwrapped, and I believe I felt it would have been worth a skinned knee to have finally tasted some (poor child of the Depression). I think Bruce did give us all a taste.

A diversion we enjoyed (at least I did) was what we called "going side track". A number of mounds of soil had been pushed up by the grader between the road and fences and we would get speed up and go bumping up and down, flying over them. The best was where a sizable hole had been dug, about nine or 10 feet from one lip to the other. Once again we got speed up, pedalled like mad, took off, flew through the air and landed on the other side, which was a little lower. No wonder I remember it seventy odd years later. Were we pioneers in mountain biking? Great fun!

In 1941 our new teacher was Eric King. By then I had caught up with Elaine and we were working together to do our Intermediate Certificate in 1943. I didn't have the best start to the year. In early March, I was in such pain I had trouble riding the last half mile home. As a result, my appendix was removed by Dr Quilter on Wednesday 12th March 1941, cost 15 pounds, fifteen shillings. Mum had exhorted me to "Be Brave" and as I waited for the anaesthetic—which was pretty horrible in those days—I prayed constantly "Dear God, help me to be brave, please make me brave". Some ladies in the ward had told me to keep still and not to move around and I obeyed them to the letter. As a result, when the time came for me to get out of bed and walk, I had to learn walking all over again, it seemed. I was so weak after two weeks' immobility.

Home at last, I was very much the invalid. Aunty Dot and Uncle Arthur Parker had been holidaying with us and took me back with them by train on the 14th April for a holiday at Belmore. They did their best to give me a good time and I put on weight. Auntie Hazel, Uncle George and Carmen were holidaying there too. Aunties Stella, Hazel and Dot took turns taking me out and about. In letters written home to my parents and sister, I wrote of having been taken to visit Aunty Stella's best friend at Bellevue Hill, Mrs Watkins, looking at shops, riding escalators and buying a skirt that was navy blue and permanently pleated at David Jones. We also had a look at Hyde Park, the Anzac Memorial, the Museum, Art Gallery, St Mary's Cathedral, St Andrew's, The Tivoli, not to mention church and Sunday School. I also enjoyed a trip on the Manly Ferry where the Hospital Boat, a Flying Boat and 'The Sydney' were pointed out to me. All around, it was a real "Cook's Tour" for a 12-year-old from the bush.

My letter, 28th April 1941: *"Uncle Arthur took me to church yesterday and Mr Connor was preaching and my did he get a surprise when he saw me. He took me to his place for dinner and I went to Sunday School at Croydon Park Church."* Rev. Connor was a loved minister in the Grenfell circuit, 1929 to 1932.

I returned by train on the 29th April accompanied by Aunty Betty and cousins, Ross and Jill, who had been in Sydney spending time with her parents. It was the 20th May before I returned to school, after having missed over two months. Elaine and I were using material from the Correspondence School, the difference being we didn't correspond; Mr King corrected our work. We were limited in our choices of subjects; no Chemistry or Language of course, but we did do English, History, Maths, Art and Business Principles.

On the King's Birthday holiday, the 15th June 1942, Elaine and I had a new experience. Our Grandfather owned an old half-Arab horse named Bill, and we went up to Spring Vale in the afternoon and rode him, in a fashion it must be admitted. Our cousin Edith was there too, and she at least knew about horses—the Grays had some and she drove a horse and sulky to school at Greenethorpe. Elaine and I were at our cowboy mad stage and did our best with our limited resources to dress suitably for the occasion. I wore gumboots on my feet which I fondly imagined looked like riding boots, a black silk bolero which had been part of the costume for an act we did for a concert (*"Come and be a Gypsy"*), a straw hat, kerchief knotted around my neck, and the final touch, a very untidy coil of rope on the pommel. All ready for roping and tying except that dear old Bill took a bit of persuasion to make him move at all. Ki Yi Yippee I Ay!

Riding "Bill" at Spring Vale.

At the end of November 1943, Elaine and I boarded in Grenfell with a family friend, Mrs Clements, and sat for the Intermediate Certificate. Mum didn't mention it again, but I passed with B's in English, History and Art, and an A in Music but unfortunately

Elaine did not. The first oblique reference was in May 1944, when she wrote: '*Beryl is boarding in Grenfell and going to High School*'.

I think that after years of recording our results in Sunday School exams, Practical and Theoretical Piano, Health and Temperance exams, with Elaine and I doing all the same things together, Mum just couldn't bring herself to write that I had succeeded and Elaine hadn't. Mr Smith had kept Elaine back so Stella Pfeiffer could be in the same class. Elaine got in the habit of doodling, drawing when she should have been getting something written on paper. It is quite possible that when she came to do the Intermediate that she didn't finish some of the questions.

Music Lessons with Miss Procter

There was a lot happening in the community known as Cowra Road, stretching perhaps six miles east and the same west and slightly less south from the Cowra Road church. There was a cricket pitch in a paddock near Brundah Creek owned by the Hopes (I think) and tennis courts in the opposite direction soon after crossing the Bungalong Creek. There was a tennis court at Spring Vale when all the family were young too but as years went by it was no longer maintained.

My Dad, I have been told, was a very good wicket keeper, and I know he had an amazing tennis serve that struck terror into the heart of the person on the other side of the net who had to receive it. But music won; Dad gave up sport to take Elaine and I to town on Saturdays for our music lessons. I had started learning piano with Miss Con Procter in late 1941 and I will now quote from my Mother's journal: "*Beryl went for her first music exam Grade 5 on the 25th of September, she was very nervous when she left home, but came home quite happy. The examiner, a Russian gentleman was very nice, and she met some nice children her own age. She got 71 marks which Miss Procter considered good, when you remember she has only had one year's tuition with Miss Procter and missed a grade, she really plays very nicely. The examiner says she has a graceful touch."* The music grades started at Six going to One then; years later that was reversed.

Miss Con Procter was a well-groomed lady; tall, thin, perhaps in her late forties or a little more when I commenced lessons in late Spring 1941. In the winter she often wore hand-knitted suits made from reasonably fine wool. I remember one suit of maroon, which contrasted well with her silver, sometimes blue-rinsed, hair. Her piano was a Lipp and we looked forward to her sometimes playing a little on it to demonstrate just how some passages should be played. That didn't happen very often; her poor knuckles were sore and swollen with rheumatism. She invariably had a beautiful big arrangement of flowers on a table in her studio, often containing flowers we didn't grow—clarkia, godetia, heuchera and others, all combining most artistically.

She always had a Scotch terrier named Scotty. When one died, he would be replaced by a lookalike, also Scotty. The one I saw most often sat in an armchair quite close to the piano and, depending on what he had been eating I suppose; his breath was somewhat, well, distracting.

I continued studying with Miss Procter doing all the Theory and Practical A.M.E.B examinations up to Grade One (which was the highest then), which I passed with credit in 1947. One year later I tried for the AMusA Associate in Music Australia, but just missed out by a hairsbreadth it seems. One had to have two examiners; one of them turned up again at Miss Procter's next year and wanted to know why "the redhead" wasn't there trying again. It seems they hovered on the edge of saying yes but they thought perhaps a little more polish was desirable so said no. Miss Procter thought if it was that close they should have taken into consideration a country student's isolation from opportunities to hear world-class artists, and given a different verdict.

1944: My Year at Grenfell Intermediate High School

After a family conference at Spring Vale, it was agreed I could have a year at Grenfell Intermediate High School. Some of the other parents between us and Greenethorpe took turns at picking the students up on Monday morning and driving them to Greenethorpe Railway Station to catch the train, and picking them up again Friday afternoon. It was still wartime and petrol rationing was in place. Along the way we would stop and take on more students at Brundah, Mogongong, Wirega and Quandong, eventually getting there in time for school. I had obtained board with Mrs Becky Armstrong whose house was second from the lower end of Middle Street on the South side, so I was under her care from Monday dinnertime to Friday afternoon tea time. She was a good cook and kind to me.

Scholastically, the year wasn't going to make any difference to the direction my life was to take, but it was good for me to be out and mixing in a wider circle and having friends of my own age.

Fourth and Fifth Years shared the same room with only four students in each. In my year there were Alwyn Frazer, Keith Briggs, David Bates and myself, while in Fifth Year there were Marie Walton, Pat Simpson, George Coroneo and Margaret Walker. Two other girls started Fourth Year but left quite early in the year. Obviously I wasn't going to do Latin, French or Chemistry, so my subjects remained the same, except that Business Principles and Bookkeeping became Economics.

One afternoon I went with some girlfriends to an area of Grenfell I hadn't been before, (I think it is now called Memory Lane—how apt) where there was an old, old house occupied by an old lady named Topsy, who wore old-fashioned clothes and told fortunes. The others had theirs told, rightly or wrongly I do not know, but I was too conscious of my parents' shadow behind me; they would *not* have approved, so I declined.

As the end of the year approached, Mum was in hospital in Young. Dutiful daughter that I was, I wrote a number of letters, mostly about splitting my sides laughing at the boys' antics and witticisms but in one I wrote, *"Elaine and Aunty Mavis called and asked me if I would like to go to the pictures so I went. Their names were* Naughty Marietta *with Jeanette McDonald and Nelson Eddy and* Hey Sailor. *Both pictures were great, there was lots of singing and Grandma shouted us!"* Thank-you Grandma.

In another letter that is before me now: *"We have been busy fixing things up for the banquet. There is such a lot to do, I have to make a speech thanking Third Year for their toast to us. This banquet is a very important affair, all the talk is of dress, shoes, hairdos and everything else that goes to make the beautiful girl. Sometimes I think I would like to get my hair cut and done nicely because it gets in the road, is hot and often doesn't look much, but I would hate parting with it I expect. It* would *look lovely done, though, and I hear Miss Curle is very good."*

Mum's reply was: *"I hope you enjoy the banquet and make a good speech, dear. I like you to look nice dear, as you know, but I don't want you to put looks first to think of little else, as some girls do, still I don't think I need be afraid, you have too much good sense!"*

Dear Mum! I doubt that being told I had too much good sense to be thinking about my appearance—which was pretty natural for a 15-year-old in the circumstances—was very helpful to me at that time of my life. Mum did have a lovely complexion, even though the only face cream she ever used was Ponds Cold Cream occasionally. She never owned a lipstick and did her hair in a style that suited her perfectly, a bun on the neck from 16-years-old until she died in her ninety-first year.

Of course Elaine and I had never learned to dance or even been allowed to stay and watch the dances that often took place after a Red Cross or Comforts fundraiser at which we had performed earlier. So after the banquet came the dance, where a nice boy asked me to dance and instead of saying, "Thank you, I'm sorry I can't dance," or "I'm game if you are," I refused him. I still remember the look he gave me when a few minutes later I was asked by someone else, and in desperation, accepted the invitation. I still feel sorry for the girl that was me.

The Court of Injustice

My one extracurricular activity was a Club our new pastor Lionel O'Dempsey started for young people, many of whom had already left school. We were divided into two teams, gold and purple, often competing against each other. One activity was a Court of Injustice where some faced charges, others were their lawyers and the rest I suppose jurors. My lawyer was Joan Hartwig, (later Joan Bernard) and the charge was sabotage of the Gold's efforts on the 25th October 1944. I had handed over the playing of the piano at a concert to Cedric Watt (thereby spoiling their chances). I was a member of the Purple team. I was found guilty of course and the penalty was to kiss the ugliest man in the room. I kissed Mr O'Dempsey's hand. Miss Flanagan was charged with cruelty to animals—presumably her pupils.

Everyone in the building screamed laughing for about five minutes when Mr O'Dempsey's case came on. The charge was "Baptising a baby upside down and so upsetting its equilibrium". The reason for the laughter was that Maurice traipsed in dressed as the mother, with a yellow and brown knitted dress, earrings, a scarf around his head, rouge and lipstick, and stockings, and you can imagine how he looked for he was 6'4" and well built. The baby in his arms was Chick (Sylvia Watt) and she had on a blue and white checked dress and bonnet and was wrapped in a shawl. The Father was Marj Walton and she had on a brown hat, trousers and coat, and a moustache, and as she would only be five feet tall, you can imagine how the two looked. He was found guilty and had to dance the sailor's hornpipe. Mr Proctor was judge and was in his glory; he had a great time.

After Sausage Curls

I changed to doing my hair in two plaits the year I attended Grenfell Intermediate High School when I was 15 and, sometime the next year I think; persuaded Mum to let me have it shortened somewhat. Our next door neighbour Mrs Stan Thompson had been a hairdresser at some time, so we walked over there and the deed was done. I think my mother didn't want to let her little girls grow up. Or perhaps she was remembering what an old aboriginal lady, black as she could be, who had come to our house and on seeing my luxuriant, glowing head of hair had said to her: "Don't you ever let anyone put scissors to that hair!"

So, my year at G.I.H.S. is behind me; *what now?* I am used to having most of my decisions made for me. Nothing has changed apart from the fact that I am no longer a school student—weekly music lessons continued for probably four more years, and Church and Sunday School as before.

We used to listen to Dr. A.E. Floyd hosting *The Music Lover's Hour* on Sunday nights and he seemed to be such a lovable, gifted person that sometimes in daydreams I thought it would be wonderful to be able to go to Melbourne and study the organ under him. He was a renowned church music composer, and organist and master of choristers at St Paul's Cathedral for 32 years after having been selected in 1915 from a field of 200 applicants. His radio program ran for more than 25 years. There was never the slightest chance of this happening but didn't I make a good choice.

★★★★

There was always a cat: Dora (short for Adorable)

One day early in 1970, when shopping in our local greengrocer's, I saw a lovely silvery-grey kitten that reminded me of Barney, and told the owners that if they were ever looking for a home for one like that, I could be interested.

A few weeks later they told me they had a kitten for me— well, she was a bit past being a kitten which she proved by having kittens herself before too long. One day she must have felt the cares of motherhood a bit heavy and that she needed time to herself, so, one by one she carried her three kittens from their bed on the front verandah around to the back door. Then she asked to be let inside and settled them down by the fireplace in the dining room.

I was touched that she trusted me to look after her precious babies during her absence. We decided it would be best if there were no more kittens, so sent her to the vet at Forbes for an operation. We were shocked and saddened when they phoned to say she had died during the operation. She had seemed nervous and had been given more anaesthetic. Poor, dear little Dora.

Over the years we lived at Cumnock Farm—1966-1994— many cats came and went. Practically all of them came and found us and made it clear they would like to stay.

One of these was **Ambrose**, a beautiful white Persian who just appeared one day in 1975 and was quite domesticated and tame so very welcome. We all loved him but didn't have the pleasure of his company as long as we should have as there were problems with a tooth. The vet at Cowra took it out but there were complications and he advised euthanasia. That was hard for all of us.

Ambrose.

Blob was another 'home grown' cat and he earned his name by often just staying 'put' where his mother plonked him down in a rather shapeless heap or 'blob'. He was black with a little white bib, born on 29 April 1969, and much enjoyed by our children being a very well behaved cat. He was one who died a natural death of old age.

Percy was born on the farm, a very gentle-natured boy. He had two sisters who used to boss him and get most of the food in their plate but he grew into a very handsome yellow-and-gold-striped cat. My son-in-law Simon once said "he looks like a Percy". I gave him that name because I thought it suited him too. In a photograph dated April 1988, I am seated in a lounge chair reading a bedtime story to my granddaughter Linda and Percy, who are both seated on my lap, Linda with one arm around Percy's neck. I think Percy is enjoying the story more than Linda, who looks very sleepy.

Percy, Linda and I.

Once again, his life wasn't as long as we would have liked. I remember one summer afternoon we were having a rest together on a seat in the garden, enjoying each other's company, and then it was time to go inside and do my chores. That was the last time any of us saw him. Whether a snake killed him or some other misadventure befell him we will never know.

Peppi was also born at Cumnock Farm and had a good thick coat of fur which appeared to be black but when parted was grey underneath and actually black tipped. I was very fond of Peppi, a most agreeable cat.

Peppi.

In July and August 1984, George and I spent nearly nine weeks overseas. Our last night in London, before boarding the plane for home next day, George phoned David to see how things were there and learned that Peppi had died at the vet's from complications after a urinary tract infection. I was quite upset as I had been looking forward to seeing him again and I am afraid most of the last couple of days of the trip home via Hong Kong were a blur to me.

★★★★

Christmas

Christmas was always spent at my Father's parents' home Spring Vale, apart from one year when we went to my Mother's old home at Temora. That was Christmas 1943, so Elaine would have been 17 and I almost 14, long past the Santa Claus stage. I know Mum would have loved to have had a Christmas there when we were little so that her grandmother, sisters and brothers could have shared in the joy of seeing us find what Santa had brought us, but that didn't happen. My great-grandmother—Nana as we called her—was there, well and very pleased to see us according to Mum's journal, but it was to be her last Christmas. She died on the 24th of June 1944, two days after her 95th birthday. Aunty Dot and Uncle Arthur were also there looking after her, and Uncle Harry was home from the Army on seasonal leave. My main memory is of being awakened by carol singers at 5:30am Christmas morning and thinking how lovely it sounded.

[Note: Offspring were scarce in Mum's family, Dot and Arthur—none, Stella and Bob—none, Harry and Teresa—none, George and Hazel—three, Alice and Norm—adopted two. There must have been some surprise among the Kings when I had six children.]

When my grandfather moved from 'Green Hills' in 1908 he built a slab house, 'Spring Vale', for his family, which included seven children (and soon to be eight). By 1920 he was affluent enough to build a large brick home on the property, complete with a gas lighting system, so there was no longer the need to rely on lamps and candles.

Spring Vale, my Father's home before he married, was like a second home to us. We stayed there when Mum had operations or wasn't well, and would sometimes call in there on our way home from school and be given lunch cakes to eat.

My grandfather, Pa as we all knew him, was very interested in public affairs, Farmers and Settlers, and local government. This was before the Country and Town amalgamation, and my Grandfather was a Shire councillor for 22 years, including Shire President, the equivalent of Mayor, for 21 years.

A trip to the lavatory at Spring Vale gave the opportunity for some reading such as you would not get anywhere else I am sure. Not the *Grenfell Record* or *The Land*, but Hansard, so as a part of our education we could read every word spoken in Parliament; and naturally what we searched for and enjoyed were the thrust and parry of debate and insults that were traded across the floor.

Christmas at Spring Vale was a big gathering of the Clan. My Grandfather expected everyone to be there—the only exception being eldest son Clarry and his wife Alice, sons Keith and Ernest, and daughter Marie. Clarry was a Methodist minister and his job, plus distance, made it well-nigh impossible. He had been at Cobar but when they moved to Ariah Park near Temora they were able to join us for dinner one year. Funny how little things stick in one's head; that year they were going to bring the tomatoes for all, and perhaps they were last to arrive because I remember the welcome, laughter and pretended relief that the TOMATOES had come!

Cuddling Barney (4th from right) for a family
photograph after dinner at Spring Vale

All brought some contribution towards the feast: Aunty Betty
brought the beetroot, my Mother dressed and cooked two lovely
big cockerels, and dear Aunty Ruby who was noted for "running
on time" if not behind, I chiefly remember as arranging flowers,
mostly carnations, still at it when it was just about time to be
seated. I am sure she did more than that; she probably brought
some sweets and nuts.

Thanks to God for food was always said in our families, and
on special occasions such as Mothers Day and Christmas it would
be sung, from the heart and in four-part harmony before eating:

> *Be present at our table Lord*
> *Be here and everywhere adored*
> *These mercies bless and grant that we*
> *May feast in Paradise with Thee.*
> *[Tune-Old 100-Doxology]*

Our menu was simple and always the same; beetroot, shredded lettuce, tomatoes, cucumber, poultry, and ham, the latter home-cured by my grandfather with much rubbing of saltpetre and brown sugar. I don't expect to taste such superlative ham ever again.

Second course was plum pudding served with white sauce, not to mention threepenny and sixpenny coins and lucky charms contained in it. The pudding was carried in and placed in front of Pa and Grandma at the head of the big table. Grandma served it with white sauce on plates that were passed around, Pa keeping a kindly eye on the plate's destination and trying to hide a coin in a plate which didn't appear to have one, especially if it was going to a grandchild. One year I found a little silver donkey but hid it as I didn't want to be called a donkey by some of the cousins. A couple of the boys would sometimes ask for a second helping and dig around in it hoping for money and not eating much. That was frowned upon as, understandably, *waste not, want not* was a maxim we all grew up with.

Grandma liked to take charge of the making of the pudding, assisted by daughters Mavis and Eva. I rode my bike up one year to watch the whole process and hopefully learn something. I remember dear Grandma rubbing the shortening and flour with her fingers and telling me to do that until it looked like breadcrumbs. Once all ingredients were mixed came the tricky bits, placing the contents of the bowl in the centre of a big square of unbleached calico (the pudding cloth), and gathering up all the outside, taking care to make the pleats as even as one could and tying together at the top with string, wound around several times and tied very tightly. Now, that was a job for more than one pair of hands. It was then lowered into the ready container of boiling water to boil for approximately six hours, the level of water being topped up with more hot water if needed. When cooked, a loop was made by tying ends of the cloth or more string and it was suspended in the pantry in a fly gauze cupboard till needed.

Grandma's pudding was always delicious. I have the recipe; why is it that I have never made it? Just another of those unanswerable questions. I have made one following my own mother's recipe which was perhaps better, definitely richer. I'll tell myself that is the reason.

After the washing up was done it was time for the gift giving or "presents" as we called it. The presents were mostly something practical; I can remember Mum checking with Dad as to the chest and shoe size of some of the uncles. I think they would probably receive white Chesty Bonds singlets one year and socks the next. We would all sit in our places around the table again and parcels were distributed by the givers, five or six probably as they were always "From all at 'Wywurry''', all at 'Renown', all at 'Spring Vale' and so on.

Sometimes a gift which wasn't strictly practical was given, such as a new game or toy that all could enjoy watching during the afternoon. One such was given to my sister Elaine at her first Christmas. It was a wind-up toy, a boy who was seated on a swing where he did amazing acrobatic feats, tumbling, somersaults, sometimes going up right over the framework above him. I'm told the Aunts and Uncles had a lovely time with Patrick, as he became known, that afternoon. Well, Elaine was only four months old. He will still perform for us, but with less enthusiasm and agility than he did 84 years ago. (Me too.)

My stand out year was 1939 when I suddenly became the focus of all eyes as I opened a shoe box which contained a most beautiful blue-gray half-Persian kitten, given to me by Aunty Pearl and Uncle Frank Gray. It was love at first sight. I named him Barney within a day or so.

After presents were packed up people were free to have a lie down if that was what they needed, get in groups and catch up on news, and make a pilgrimage out to the laundry that was part of the old house. At Christmas it contained a barrel of ginger beer made by my Grandmother and which was invariably a terrific brew. Non-alcoholic of course, but it was observed one year that two uncles, Claude Wales and Frank Gray; who like us all appreciated it, but perhaps had just a little more than their share, became just noticeably relaxed and giggly. A few glances were exchanged.

As far as I know, no one in the family ever thought to get Grandma's recipe. What an omission. A pity!

Late in the afternoon some would gather in the kitchen and make a big bowl of fruit salad to be enjoyed at the evening meal.

During the evening there would be a "sing" and family members were encouraged to contribute items which had been their speciality over the years. Aunty Eva could sing alto, but was mostly at the piano or organ as accompanist, Uncle Selby was a gifted player of the musical saw, and Aunty Pearl and Uncle Frank sang duets. Aunty Ruby had a lovely contralto voice and incidentally, we enjoyed it again in 1983 when she and her twin sister's daughter, Betty, sang *Just a Song at Twilight* at my parents' Diamond Wedding celebration. Uncle Clarry's special song was Longfellow's *The Arrow and the Song*, while Uncle Arthur and my Dad had three duets I particularly remember: *Larwood Watch*, *The Army and the Navy* and *Excelsior*, words by Longfellow. Grandma and Aunty Mavis had good voices for leading the soprano in the four-part harmony, while Pa Pereira sat in his easy chair, not singing very much but beaming with pleasure and pride in his family.

More about the Ham

I guess Pa bought a pig from a neighbour in autumn as we didn't breed them. As my Dad was the best shot he had the job of shooting it. I think this would have been in the winter when there was a frost. We would be given some meat but the two legs were reserved to be treated with brown sugar, saltpetre and I don't know what else to be made into hams. One was for Christmas and one was for sandwiches for the Methodist Quarterly Meeting which was held in the Cowra Road Church once a year with afternoon tea at Spring Vale. The importance of this event can be gauged by the fact that it merited one ham. The ladies were entertained at Spring Vale while keeping an eye out for the arrival of the minister and men who had been involved in the business of the Quarterly Meeting. No ladies were permitted in that august assembly in those days! Very few visitors to Spring Vale knocked at the front door; they followed the road that led to the back gate and entered there. To me, seeing the cars drive slowly up the driveway and stopping at the FRONT GATE, then watching as these important looking men of serious mien, dressed in their dark suits walk up with dignity to the front door, certainly made an impression and almost inspired awe. Maybe they *did* deserve our second ham for their sandwiches after all.

Something else made a big impression on me that day too. I was of an age to be interested in romance and one of the ladies in the kitchen was a recent bride, Sadie Diprose, who was a very good cook. She had baked a lovely chocolate sponge and when the time came to open the cornflakes box she thought she had carried it in, there was *no cake*, just what the label said, cornflakes. There was much laughter and no doubt Ron was the lucky one to enjoy the cake.

A Brief Family History

Grace

My mother was born in Temora to Walter and Ada King nee Foulkes on the 20th January 1897. Walter came from an athletic family, and in his young days had acquired a considerable reputation as a foot runner and pole vaulter, at both of which he excelled.

I don't know anything about Ada's life before marriage, though we have quite a lot about her mother Emma, "Nana" Foulkes. My mother's time at school was often not very happy from what she told me a long, long time ago, with some teachers very quick with a rap across the knuckles for an incorrect answer. So, I think she left school as soon as was allowed and I believe she worked for a dressmaker nearby, helping with plain sewing. That could have come later however, as by that time three sisters and two brothers had been added to the family and no doubt her mother needed her help on the domestic scene.

Sadly, Ada died from pneumonia before her 40th birthday and from then Grace, at the age of 16, took on the role of mother, to the best of her ability, to her siblings, the youngest of whom was George, only five years old. They were always a very close, caring family. Years and years later, when Mum had been married 15-20 years, always after a visit to Temora and after we had said our goodbyes to whoever was there at the time, 10 or more miles on the way home Elaine and I in the back seat of the car would note Mum still wiping the tears away, and give each other a look. I always thought "she has <u>us</u>, why is she crying?"

We often have a smile when reading old letters or a journal of hers, to see orchard always spelt orchid; and to read that "*Beryl and George dropped in for a few minuets after church*". Can you picture it?

She read a lot and was very discerning in her knowledge and judgements of world events and people. My sister Elaine used to sometimes, only half joking, call her a witch! One of Mum's sayings was "I just face facts". And she had to, all her life.

The Spring Vale clan on a shooting trip at Brundah:
Alfred, George Henley Pereira, Charlotte, Ruby,
Eva, Pearl, Grace and Mavis.

I was always proud of the way she could converse with some of our visitors, the minister for instance, on really heavy subjects and felt that in spite of the lack of formal education and her wrestling with spelling she really was an educated lady. We were taught to appreciate and treasure books. It was a tradition to read *The Night Before Christmas* aloud on Christmas Eve when we were little, and later the account of Christmas at Elsey Station from *We of the Never Never* by Mrs Aeneas Gunn. We also of course read the entire book and some of the books by L.M. Montgomery, especially the *Anne* books. Other books shared were *Cranford* by Mrs Gaskell, *Alice in Wonderland* by Lewis Carroll, *Little Women* and *Good Wives* by Louisa M. Alcott, J. Bunyan's *Pilgrims Progress* (Arthur Mee's version for children), and *The Vanished World of Yesterday* by Lord Frederick Hamilton.

Mum had a very good soprano voice and did a considerable amount of solo and choral work both before and after marriage. On the domestic scene the two specialities I particularly remember were apple pie and a richly flavoured vegetable soup. Mother heard my prayers at bedtime, which I suppose were very much of the "God bless Mummy and Daddy, God bless Elaine and help me to be a good girl" variety, but I do remember her singing an old hymn for children:

> *Jesus, tender Shepherd, hear me;*
> *Bless thy little lamb tonight;*
> *Through the darkness be Thou near me;*
> *Keep me safe till morning light.*

> *All this day thy hand has led me,*
> *And I thank Thee for Thy care;*
> *Thou hast clothed me, warmed and fed me;*
> *Listen to my evening prayer.*

> *Let my sins be all forgiven;*
> *bless the friends I love so well;*
> *Take me, when I die to heaven,*
> *Happy there with Thee to dwell.*

Often, when awake at night, wishing I was asleep, I mentally sing it to myself, the only difference being that in the second line of the last verse I substitute "ones" for "friends", thinking of my dear family. My Mother's best friend Nell Hughes in a letter to her early in 1985 soon after Dad's death enclosed a little card that said:

If you can't sleep don't count sheep, talk to the Shepherd.

Grace and her siblings

Ethel **Grace** King—20/1/1897-21/10/1987

Stella Annie Emma—20/8/1899-20/10/1962, sometimes just "Stelle" or "Em". Aunty Stella worked in O'Gilpin's shop and became manageress. Married to Robert Harvey (Bob).

Alice Lillian—28/9/1901-27/12/1980, had auburn hair so was sometimes called "Blue". At some stage she decided to spell her name Alyce—same person however spelt. Aunty Alice gained enough qualification to be accepted as a teacher at small schools where the parents also contributed. She taught in the Condobolin area and for Caldwell's on Nambucca Station.

Walter Henry (Harry)—30/1/1904-19/12/1973, also known in the cycling world as "Lob".

Ada Ernestine (Dot)—3/8/1905-15/9/1993, Dot called so because some playmates said "You're such a little dot" and Dot she was ever after. Dot worked in the office of a butcher.

George Robert—18/5/1908-13/5/1985 (Horder), also called "Horder" in a newspaper cutting entitled *'Death of Famous Athlete'* found in the King family red folder. I think Lob and Horder were names of former champions probably in cycling and were given to my uncles as a compliment.

Walter and Ada King—Mum's Parents

I didn't ever know my grandparents as Ada died from pneumonia in 1913 when Mum was 16, and Walter died in 1929, the year I was born, but I feel I do know them in some way from the few photos we have. There is a good one of Walter taken 11 months before he died; wearing a suit, well groomed and seated in a chair; one hand resting on his leg, the other on the arm of the chair. His hands are the honest hands of a working man. I have been told my Dad said: *"He was a good bloke"*. That was high praise.

The other photo is one taken on their wedding day, both in navy Salvation Army uniform; he seated, Ada standing with hand on his shoulder, both serious, looking at the camera. The touch that still amuses me was the white sash Ada wore; coming over her right shoulder and tied near her waist on the left with the words SIMPLY TRUSTING in large print across it.

Part of his obituary in the *Temora Independent* Thursday, 3rd October, 1929 is as follows:

A native of Yorktown, SA, he came to Temora about forty years ago (i.e. late 1880's) and was one who took part in the stirring scenes enacted here when the fame of the Temora goldfields had spread throughout the State.

His first experience of mining operations here was at Reefton, and later he followed this pursuit with indifferent success at Temora.

He came from an athletic family, and in his young days had acquired a considerable reputation as a foot-runner and pole vaulter, at both of which athletics he excelled. He is a brother of the well-known foot-runner, Jimmy King of Eaglehawk, Victoria and his other surviving brother, Arthur, of Cowra was a first class cyclist in his day.

Possessing a kindly and genial nature, with a ready sympathy and willingness at all times to help anyone in a less fortunate position than himself, he had, during his long residence here, gathered round him a coterie of friends of such proportions as to make him one of the best known and popular residents in the town.

He was one of the oldest members of the local Order of the Manchester Unity Oddfellows, having joined 30 years ago, and been a useful and loyal member ever since. In his demise the Salvation Army loses a devout and loyal and staunch supporter, and the manner in which he attended to his religious duties was an inspiration to all who knew him.

Nana—My Great Grandmother— Emma Brown

Nana's father, John Brown was a soldier in the Grenadier Guards and was first posted to Ireland, followed by Van Dieman's Land (Tasmania) and then Sydney. While in Sydney he married Maria Reece, who was Welsh, and in due course Emma was born in the Married Soldiers Barracks on 22nd June, 1849.

Maria loved this sunny land of Australia and didn't want to leave it, so John obtained his discharge from the Army and joined the Police Force, but didn't continue there for very long. It was the time of the bad old rum days and he hated having to deal with drunken men in the gutters, feeling it was beneath his dignity.

He then acquired some land near Wollongong and, knowing nothing about clearing it, one of the first things he did was to fell a tree on top of himself and was killed. Emma's mother was left with two little girls in a strange land. After a time she married again.

Emma attended a school which was run by the Rector's daughter. This cost her mother two shillings and sixpence (25 cents) a week. We have a photo of Emma taken at the age of seventeen. She is wearing a dress she had made herself, long full skirt trailing a little at the back, sleeves ruched at the top—quite likely made without a pattern. In the photo she is posing with a serious and confident expression on her face. Well may she have this demeanour as she had left school at the age of 12 and straightaway gone out to work as a maid and be responsible for herself. Imagine it!

One of the families she worked for was the Chisholm family who lived near Goulburn. They were a well-to-do family 'of quality' and treated her very well. The servants were required to join the family for prayers every morning. She stayed with the Chisholms for years and then, with a married daughter of the Chisholm's, went to live near the Fish River.

Once when she was working for a wealthy family, bushrangers came; left their tired horses and made off with the family's race horses. Another time, she told the story of when the Kelly gang had to flee from a hotel because the police were on their tracks, the maids found a gift of a bottle of perfume in their room.

At one place where she worked, she was allowed to ride a horse. She used to practise jumping over fallen logs but in her own words she "often went over before the horse did".

When she was almost 23 years old, Emma Brown was married to George Foulkes at the Holy Trinity Church of England in Grenfell on the 18th April, 1872. George owned a bullock team which was 'something' in those days. Emma had 10 pounds and a trunk full of clothes.

After some time the bullock team was sold and a good horse and spring cart were bought. George had a sawmill and made timber pickets for fences. He followed the lure of gold mining for many years but didn't make his fortune, just payable gold, enough to keep going. Emma said she could have made more money with a store, selling things to the miners.

At one time when they were at Reefton near Temora, Emma owned the only sewing machine on the diggings. It was turned by hand and Emma said she sewed up miles of unbleached calico for women who wanted to line their little homes, as well as for her own home.

When a Minister came riding on horseback to the diggings, she was asked to put him up for the night as she was the only one whose home was lined at that time. Her home was quite large for the times and made of big sheets of bark on both walls and roof.

George died on 21st September, 1918.

Nana Foulkes with our family.

In all my memories of Nana, she was in her eighties and nineties, tall and slim, long silver hair with a natural wave and worn in a bun. I remember her well as she lived in the family home at Temora with Uncle Harry until he was called up into the army, Aunty Dot till she married in 1936 and Aunty Alice until she married in 1939. Aunty Dot and Uncle Arthur returned to Temora from Sydney in April, 1942 and she lived with them until her death. Nana was always dressed in black perhaps relieved by wearing a white jabot fastened at the throat by a cameo brooch, or as a concession to the summer heat of Temora; a white blouse with a black skirt. We have a photo of her on the verandah telling Elaine and I stories of her encounters with bushrangers.

For relaxation she enjoyed a good detective story and doing crochet, and we have many pieces of her work. She had a wonderful attitude towards life and a keen sense of humour. When a Minister called during a heat wave and asked how she was standing up to it her reply was, "Lying down, mostly".

One day during the second World War, looking around she said, "This is a beautiful country and worth fighting for".

She died at Temora on 24th June, 1944, just two days after her ninety-fifth birthday.

World War Two:
3rd September 1939-10th August 1945

After years of the Depression, life changed again when the war started on the 3rd September 1939. Rationing commenced for sugar, tea, butter, clothing and petrol. Petrol rationing didn't finish until 1949.

My ration card.

Dad and his brother Arthur each bought a piano-accordion and joined the Grenfell Musical Orchestral, Vocal Society and later The Grenfell District Entertainers. They helped entertain the soldiers in Cowra Army Camp and raised funds for comforts for the troops, and the Red Cross. Music changed, with titles like: *There'll Always Be An England*, *Kiss Me Goodnight Sergeant Major*, and *Coming In On A Wing and a Prayer*.

> *"Kiss Me Goodnight Sergeant Major Tuck me in my little wooden bed.*
> *We all love you Sergeant-Major When we hear you calling 'Show a leg.'*
> *Don't forget to wake me in the morning Bring me round a nice hot cup of tea;*
> *Kiss me goodnight, Sergeant-Major Sergeant-Major, be a mother to me."*

> *"Coming in on a wing and a prayer, Coming in on a wing and a prayer,*
> *With our full crew on board and our trust in the Lord;*
> *We're coming in on a wing and a prayer.*
> *What a show, what a fight, Yes we really hit the target tonight."*

Thinking of wartime music reminded me of another song— *When the lights come on again all over the world*, and that in turn reminded me of the blackouts. It didn't concern us as these were the years before electricity came our way and our lights were lamps and candles, but in cities and potential target towns blackout material had to be purchased and made into curtains which would not permit a chink of light to be visible outside. Air raid wardens would patrol to check all was as it should be.

Some people dug air raid shelters in their back yards. At Temora Uncle Harry converted what had been an underground well into one by cutting steps down into it and making an entrance. I remember clambering down into it one time, full of anticipation—I think I felt it would be an interesting variation of a cubby house. There were a few things down there; a table, lamp, matches, torch, biscuits and CHOCOLATE. I don't remember other things, but had the war come closer at that time there would have been chairs, rugs etc.

Of course big cities were potential targets of the enemy, but Temora did have an Air Force pilot training school, so who knows? We used to watch the planes flying and circling above and wonder what might be the fate of some of those young men up there as the war continued.

With many wartime shortages many people used to make do with innovations. One of these was charcoal burners attached to cars to overcome the petrol rationing. Dad's cousin, Wilbur Starr had one of these.

My mother kept a journal, first entry Good Friday, 11 April, 1941, so that unfortunately, we don't have her comments on the beginning of the war or the end. The first reference to war was Monday 5th May: *"We went to a welcome to our new minister Rev. Chapman. It was also a farewell to three Methodist boys, Moffitt, Woods and Mitton. Alf and Arthur sang a duet, 'The Army and the Navy' very nicely."*

Mum's journal, Friday 9th May, 1941: *"The Pfeiffer family were over Friday night and we had a nice time with music and singing and Chinese Checkers."*

I think Chinese Checkers were new to us at that time but they became an enjoyed part of our recreation. We have a continuing friendship with the Pfeiffers. George's sister Dot married Les, who had gone to school with Elaine and I. In June 2010, George and I had the pleasure of joining friends and relations at their home near Canowindra to celebrate Les's eightieth birthday. All his siblings were there: Stan, Marjorie, Stella and Thelma.

22nd May 1941: *"Alf has taken a carload to attend a First Aid Lecture by a Doctor tonight.*

We had Christmas day, at "S.V". Thankful to have had a peaceful day in a world at war. Japan started in on American and British possessions while talking peace and our country is in more danger than it has ever been. Daylight savings is to be started tomorrow."

Earlier she had written: *"School closed earlier this year as the teacher Mr King was called up for training for home defence. They had a happy little concert at the breakup. Beryl won the prize for spelling, the fourth in succession."*

She then went on to note rain was very badly needed and that her Grandmother was ill and she hoped to soon go to Temora and see her. It was typical of our lives at that time—pleasure in family achievements, concern for loved ones at home and abroad, hoping for rain, and always the war in one's mind.

25th May 1942: *"Empire day and we are still at war but still an Empire. Dreadful battles in Russia and the Japs threatening Australia as well as other countries."* Crutching and few showers.

August 1942: *"I have made two wool rugs this winter. We washed the wool very carefully, Alf teased it all and I sewed the wool onto one unbleached sheet and covered it with another sheet, and machine sewed it all over in little squares. They are lovely and warm, as warm as a pair of good blankets."*

[Note: 21st June 2011—You are so right Mum, I have one of them anchored inside a doona cover on our bed this winter and it is so cosy and warm, I snuggle in and don't want to get out of bed in the mornings.]

9th November 1942: *"The war has taken a brighter turn for the Allies at last, the eighth army has had a big victory in Africa and are chasing the remnants of Rommel's men. The Americans have had a*

Beryl Walker

Naval victory in the Solomons. Our boys are hunting the Japs out of New Guinea. Stalingrad has not fallen yet, a great convoy has landed a large American Army in Africa. The weather is hot and dry."

1942 closed with the school 'break-up' and concert at which I recited, *When Granny was a girl* and playing the guitar, accompanied Elaine, Connie Hughes and myself singing *The Umbrella Man* and *Silent Night*, in which I sang alto. My gift for Christmas was a pretty blue floral satin coat hanger. I think I gave it to my daughter Alison many years later. The Christmas pudding that was eaten New Years Day was, to quote Mum, *"mixed by Beryl and proved a beauty"*.

We often saw the dust of convoys of troops going past our home. Monday 15th March 1943: *"Lots of soldiers went by. The commanding officer, a Sergeant and another lad, returned from overseas, came in and sat in the kitchen, and talked and ate grapes and watermelon while we boiled enough hot water to make tea for forty odd soldiers who were having a rest in the creek. They have been in the hills for several days, had the weekend in Grenfell and were walking back to Cowra. Such nice lads, two of them from Tasmania."*

Monday 12th April, 1943—
Visit of Lord and Lady Wakehurst to Grenfell

As told by my mother:

"This was a great day for Grenfell and District. The State Governor, Lord Wakehurst and Lady Wakehurst visited the town.

"They seem a very fine couple, both tall, he fair and she dark. They reviewed the troops, the Volunteer Defence Corps, Scouts and Guides, the National Emergency Service, returned soldiers, CWA and Red Cross and had morning tea in the Presbyterian Hall. Pa as Shire President made a speech of welcome, as did the Mayor and the member of Parliament, Mr.

82

Cahill. His Lordship made a good speech. The speeches and welcome were held on the steps of the Shire and Municipal building.

"*They came on the train in the morning and left at half-past four in the afternoon. They were to visit the hospital, the Bowling Club and the Country Women's rooms in the afternoon. Lady Wakehurst spoke to Elaine and told her she was a young NES worker and asked her did she like it. Needless to say, it gave her a great thrill. Beryl's knee was too bad for her to put her foot properly to the ground, so she could not go with the school children but stayed with Aunty Betty where she could lean against a tree. During the morning tea the Grenfell Orchestral Society of which Alf is now a member, played several selections and then ate the crumbs that fell from His Excellency's table, and had his photo taken.*"

I have a different memory of that occasion. I was really very proud of Pa, as we called our Grandfather, but that day I was decidedly embarrassed when, in his capacity as Shire President he made a speech of welcome and referred to His Lordship as Lord WORKHASTE! Oh Paaaa.

On 2nd May 1943 we were invited to the Parsonage for the evening meal. Rev and Mrs Chapman's daughter, Mrs Sidman, was living with them while her husband who was in one of the Services, (Army, I think) was away. She played the piano beautifully for us and it was a memorable evening. Elaine and I were inspired.

The Parsonage is now our home; my piano is in the same position as hers was, and 68 years later I am enjoying spending time there with my granddaughter Grace, playing for her, listening to her with much pleasure and admiration, and learning duets together.

2nd May: "*Beryl has been sick with swollen glands and pains in the head, most of her time in bed. She has lost three weeks school, first with a sore knee hurt playing at school, then sick."* Later in May I spent time in hospital with earache. Finally my adenoids were taken out for the second time. More "being brave" on the 11th June. Mum's comment: *"Beryl is a very brave little woman!"*

Sunday 16th May 1943: *"A special thanksgiving service today for the Victory in North Africa, no Axis troops there now, except as prisoners, a wonderful victory and to God be thanks. We heard through the wireless, the bells of England pealing in thanksgiving and what joy it brought us."*

24th May 1943: *"Empire Day, the happiest since the war began, although things still are serious the outlook is brighter and our position improving. The sinking of our hospital ship by the Japanese is just what you could expect from savages."*

Mum wasn't the only one who thought like that; the Federal leader of the United Australia Party, Mr Hughes, said "the callous sinking of the Centaur will fill every Australian with horror. We are fighting against savages, not civilised men." Likewise, Sir Henry Manning said the Japanese had proved themselves a nation of savages, in the Sydney Morning Herald, 19th May 1943.

In mid-June 1943, Elaine and I each had a new winter dress. We saw them in the shop window of Western Stores and they were our size, oh joy! Elaine's was maroon with blue appliqué flowers, mine navy with white Broderie Anglaise collar and pockets embroidered with little roses. Both very stylish we felt.

Mum helps Elaine and I show off our new
winter dresses, June 1943.

Also by June 1943, Dad had joined the Grenfell Musical and
Orchestral Society so now there was no holding him. On 24th
June he took his place in the orchestra playing the cello, which
he had taught himself, playing the *Poet and Peasant Overture* and
other pieces. He also played a selection on his piano accordion.
On the 15th July there was another concert in the Brundah Hall,
this time for the Red Cross. In August, Dad, Elaine and I helped
with a musical programme at Greenethorpe in aid of the Red
Cross and Prisoner of War Funds.

2nd August 1943: *"Mussolini, the dictator of Italy has been forced
to resign and his party broken up. Italy seems in a state of unrest and
uncertainty. The Russians are doing well, so are the rest of the War
fronts.*

September 1944: *"The Grenfell District Entertainers took two good
concerts to Cowra A.I.F. [Australian Infantry Forces] Camp. Everyone
had a good time.*

October 1944: *"A concert was given for the Salvation Army in August, a good crowd in the Star Theatre (Odd fellows Hall). The army benefited by £5 ($10)."*

September 1944: *"A lot of Jap prisoners of war escaped out of Camp at Cowra and made some excitement for a while, burnt their huts down, threw their blankets over the barbed wire fence and lots escaped, over nine hundred ran amok killed a gun crew of ours before things could be got under control, things were soon in order again."*

That was my Mother's last entry for a number of years—what a pity she didn't continue for another year, I would have liked to have heard what she had to say at the end of the war. The Cowra Prisoner Of War Camp breakout occurred approximately 2am on Saturday 2nd of August 1944, with 234 Japanese killed, 108 wounded and 334 recaptured. This of course was not very far from where we lived and we were probably told to keep our eyes open and the doors were locked at night but apart from that it was taken calmly as far as we were aware. In September 1944, we saw the survivors being transported on the back of trucks past our home out to Hay. It gave one a rather shivery feeling.

Land Girls

There was an organisation called the Women's Land Army made up of women who worked on farms producing vegetables, fruit, dairy and other produce to enable men to join the fighting services.

Elaine and I had our chance to see ourselves as Land Girls, as they were known, in 1943 or 1944. It was probably when Uncle Arthur was at a Volunteer Defence Corp (V.D.C) training camp as happened quite often; and Dad being short of manpower decided Elaine and I could rake the mown Lucerne paddock into windrows ready for bailing. I was given the job of driving the tractor, Elaine operating the rake, I suppose I was given a few instructions and away we went, very pleased with ourselves. The task was completed without any hitches.

I drove the tractor while Elaine operated the rake
during the manpower shortage of 1943-44.

★★★★

There was always a cat: Tabitha

One afternoon, probably about 1988, I was standing outside the kitchen window when a cat appeared from underneath the Carob Bean trees and walked over to me. I picked her up and that was that; we had another cat—not just a cat, a loved member of our family. George happened to be watching from the kitchen sink and saw it happen. He said that she walked straight up to me, rubbed her face against my leg and clearly said that she had come to stay.

Tabitha.

She obviously hadn't been doing it hard; living off the land as best she could or recently dropped by someone. She was quite an armful with a thick fluffy coat; black and tawny markings predominating with white tummy, whiskers and bib, socks and mittens—very attractive. One day after a hard look at her I said,

"Uh huh—I think I know why you were tossed out. Are you going to have kittens?"

As time went on, no kittens arrived. One night while watching TV, I learned some vets put a tattoo inside the ear of a female feline they have neutered. I looked and quite distinctly there was a symbol tattooed—so no kittens, ever. So, her former owners had been responsible in having that taken care of.

She could be rather quick with the claws and I feel perhaps she had scratched someone after her magnificent tail had been pulled—hence her expulsion. I am always on the cat's side in these matters.

Not long before we moved to town a fox was sighted in our garden. What should we do? Brave Tabitha took charge of the situation into her paws and chased it off the premises. We were all very impressed; especially Elaine who presented her with an Award for Valour, a metal badge threaded on a bright red ribbon to be worn round the neck. It was the shape of a koala with "Killer Koala" across the chest and at its feet the words, "Stick 'em up Babe". It wasn't very big, so with a little imagination one could see the koala as a cat.

We used to have good games together in the evening with a couple of pyjama cords; she was a bundle of energy with a great deal of imagination.

She used to regularly do the rounds of the sheds hunting for mice but when we went to town or wherever, she almost invariably met us at the back gate. This even happened when we returned from two-and-a-half-months overseas in mid-1990 and she gave us a great welcome which was very touching.

We moved to 'Illoura', 33 Forbes Street, Grenfell in September, 1994. I had concerns about Tabitha's wellbeing and sure enough the first night we were here, she gave us the slip and crawled under the neighbouring preschool. George was able to retrieve her. The next day we gave her a comprehensive tour of the garden explaining the purpose of the fences and where she may and may not go.

After that all was well; although there was one time I was highly amused. I was watching as she walked down our front path, out onto the footpath, turned right and was approaching the preschool boundary fence. Time to intervene—I said, "Tabitha, just where do you think you are going?" She immediately stopped and retraced her steps, back down the footpath, through the gateway, continuing up the garden path and up the front steps. She then turned around on the edge of the verandah, deliberately sat down giving me a look that I swear said, "There, are you satisfied now?"

Sometime in 1998 we became aware she was losing weight so took her to our vet who told us she had feline aids and that nothing could be done to save her. That was a dreadful shock, she had not had encounters with other cats in our knowledge but he said it could have gone back to her former life.

Over the weeks she became frailer and unable to jump on the bed with us as she used to. It was time to part and she passed away on 26th October, 1998. We wrapped her in an old mohair jumper of mine which she loved and buried her in our Arboretum on the farm.

★★★★

Youth and Young Adulthood

While Mum often told us Dad never told her he wished he had a son or that one of the girls had been a boy; I knew nevertheless they would have liked a son.

So Dad did the best he could, bought us each a pair of khaki bib and brace overalls and from time to time we went with him to an area of the farm fenced off from stock and cropping which he called 'No Man's Land'. There we helped him in digging out bluebells. I shudder to think of it now as I love our wildflowers, but at that time the idea was that the land had to be made productive to grow grass for the sheep (not that Dad owned any as they were all Pa's).

Anyway we loved being up there in the hills—there was Crown Land over our boundary fence—and one memorable day Dad taught us how to shoot. I did quite well and from time to time kept the silver eye population down somewhat when the grapes were ripe.

Dear Dad also presented us each with a pocket knife. He also taught me to set rabbit traps and to skin rabbits, skills of little use in succeeding years, but I did enjoy spending time with my Dad in the hills behind our home.

We liked having family picnics, just on the hills visible from our house, or as happened on a couple of occasions on Boxing Day, we started from Spring Vale and all piled on the lorry driven by Uncle Arthur as far as we could go on that. We then climbed over the fence to what we called 'The Big Rock' which was on the Crown Land. We enjoyed lovely views to the south. Native ferns grew in the crevices of the rocks.

I remember one occasion when Mum, Elaine and I went down in an area we called 'Wattle Grove' up the creek near our neighbours, the Thompsons, for afternoon tea. Mum had made a new slice for the occasion and Mrs Thompson came with one of her wonderful chocolate sponges and her three little boys. It was a lovely place with wattles blooming in season, and a clear running stream with soft water weeds floating on it.

Our parents were very hospitable and frequently had family and friends for a picnic in the hills or up the creek at Wattle Grove. This was usually followed by a meal and evening of talking with music, singing and sometimes playing table tennis. Once one of the players crashed into the sideboard and while it rocked, nothing was broken or damaged! I think Dad caught some pieces. This sideboard now stands in our dining room with the very same pieces on the top shelf.

Elaine and I were expected to play something on the piano, solos and a duet as our contribution to the entertainment, and I have to regretfully record that while outwardly polite and I hope, pleasant; inwardly I would be seething and browned off because when I had played a movement of a Sonata by Mozart or a lovely Nocturne by Chopin, someone would chirp: "That's a pretty little piece!"

A family portrait.

Sometimes, too, Mum would find she had taken on a bit too much and would say "I can't cope, I can't cope" so of course I would have to abandon whatever I was doing and help (which I trust I did gladly?).

We had no electricity and this was long before the days of TV. There was wireless so, when Dad could keep the batteries charged with the wind-driven generator that he had made, we could listen to that. We always had to do our piano practice after coming home from school, so listening would have been mostly in the evenings when work was done and of course what we heard was mostly Dad's choice but we didn't have any problems with that.

That was when we first heard William Herbert singing and we became big fans. He had a beautiful tenor voice, was based in Melbourne and for some reason we had better reception with Victorian stations so listened to them. Dad even bought the Victorian *Listener In* magazine so that we could select what we wanted to hear from it.

We rarely went to the movies but enjoyed those we did see. I mentioned *Gulliver's Travels* in my account of school years. We also saw *Snow White* and *Firefly*. *Firefly* was one I remember very clearly. It starred Jeanette Macdonald as Nina Maria Azara, a beautiful and alluring singing spy for Spain during the Napoleonic Wars. The male lead was Allan Jones and I will always remember his singing of 'The Donkey Serenade' to her while seated on a horse, she in some sort of carriage being drawn along by a donkey, singing to her but sometimes pretending he was singing to the donkey. It was released in 1937, and in 1939 Mum gave Elaine a copy of 'The Donkey Serenade', so we probably saw it during that year. I still have that copy.

Sometime in 1945 we saw the film *A Song to Remember* and that definitely gave us a new vision of what a pianist could be and do. It was the story of Chopin with emphasis on his Polish patriotism which is reflected in some of his music. It was produced during World War Two. There was lots of wonderful music that we had not heard previously—remember there was no television or Music Club then. Cornel Wilde played the part of Chopin, Merle Oberon as George Sand, José Iturbe was the pianist and the hands of Ervin Nyiregylazi were shown playing the piano. We soaked up every note and revelled in the experience.

For us—back to the piano, there is much more to do yet.

Career!

There was no question of such a thing as a career for, like most girls on a farm, we were expected to stay home and help our Mother and sometimes Dad. So apart from our weekly music lessons with Miss Procter in Grenfell and hours spent practising at home, we learned how to do the washing using a copper where the bed linen sheets were boiled. Firstly, one collected wood and kindling to light the fire under it. Articles to be boiled were placed in a copper while the water was still cold along with finely cut soap (Velvet or Sunlight) and sometimes a tablet of something called 'Dad'—I remember the slogan, "Let Dad do it". They were brought to the boil—10 to 15 minutes giving a few prods from the copper stick along the way. The copper stick was wooden, round, approximately 1¼ inches (3cms) wide and 2½ feet long; long enough to keep you somewhat out of the hot steam. Next, using the copper stick, one fished the clothes out into a wooden box with holes in it where they drained before they were transferred to a cement rinsing-tub. After that to another tub with blue in it (Reckitts blue knob) if they were white, which our sheets and pillow slips always were. It didn't do to dunk pink or yellow garments into the blued water!

Reckitt's Blue was an essential part of laundry day.

No drip dry materials then, so everything was put through the wringer to get most of the water out, then into a big cane clothes basket and out to the clothes line—wire attached to posts with a wooden pole in the centre that enabled it to be raised and lowered. We had four lines in a sort of a square. Our dresses, shirts, nightwear, underwear, etc, and Dad's work clothes weren't boiled. They were scrubbed in a tub of suds on a ribbed scrubbing board, and then given the rinse treatment before pegging out with wooden pegs.

That wasn't the last of it, as things had to be brought in when dry or nearly so, aired on a clothes horse in front of the kitchen fire in winter, then folded and put away. Articles that had to be ironed were dampened. Starch (Silver Star) for things such as tablecloths, doyleys and aprons was made and used after the last rinse and wringing but these needed to be evenly damp for ironing, so they were dampened, rolled up in a towel and left for a while before ironing.

Talking of ironing—that was something else! No lightweight, gleaming appliance whose heat you could control with a touch of the switch. Once again the wood in the fuel stove provided the heat, and experience helped there. It was all too easy to scorch Dad's white Sunday shirt with a touch from an overheated iron. We had three or four cast iron irons of varying weights which heated on top of the stove and, as one cooled down while being used, you replaced it and took another, being careful to give it a rub from a clean cloth in case it transferred some black from the stove to; once again, Dad's Sunday shirt.

That reminds me of another task—blackleading and polishing the stove. Applying the liquid with a brush then buffing it off. Mum took a lot of pride in the appearance of her stove but it was a dirty job. Fine black particles flew in all directions; up one's nose, everywhere; there was quite a clean-up job to do afterwards.

Another wintertime job was whitewashing the chimney surrounding the black grate that held the fire in our dining room. Mum loved to keep it white and I remember her telling me her brother Harry (or George?) had said that when he arrived at heaven's gate he expected to be greeted by sister Stella with a broom and his sister Grace—my Mother—with a whitewash brush in her hand!

Crusader Camps

When I was 17, early in 1946; our friends Marj and Stella Pfeiffer told us of a wonderful time they had the previous Easter at a Crusader Camp meeting lots of new young people. These were under the auspices of the Methodist Church, for young people over 17, and were very well organised and held twice a year, on the Easter and October long weekends. This sounded great; would we like to go with them this Easter at Young? Would we? A resounding YES!

Up to 120 young people attended these camps held at up to a dozen sites at the same time across NSW. They were usually set up on a Showground or campsite in the country, where we slept on the floor of the pavilion or similar, on hessian bags filled with straw, not to mention the occasional thistle, and by the third night they began to feel reasonably comfortable.

The program included study periods, outings, a concert and *Humouresque*—a newspaper containing lots of laughs and gossip, real and fabricated about campers, and lots and lots more.

The program went like this: Reveille at 6.30am; Morning devotions 7.30am; Breakfast 7.45am; Camp service 9 am; Study circles 10.45am; Lunch 1pm; Afternoon free but often an organised outing. Saturday night there would be a concert—always with plenty of talent, and during the evening meal the reading of *Humouresque*, both were riotous affairs. *Humouresque* was very

97

clever when Uncle Merrick Webb—Rev. M. Webb—was editor as frequently happened.

Each morning there were study groups with a leader and perhaps seven or so others. Every study group had to have people with different gifts to offer. I filled the role of the silent member admirably.

We had Camp Mother and Father and a Chief Speaker, Boys and Girls House Committees and most importantly, a professional cook. We took turns at waitressing and were requested to be on duty 45 minutes before meal times. Lights out was supposed to be 11pm and mostly was. On the last day, Monday, there was a Communion Service before lunch, then another edition of *Humouresque*. It was then time then to pack up and head for home.

On returning home, we of course, told Mum and Dad all about it in such glowing terms that Dad decided he wasn't going to miss out and from then on went to every one! I have been asked did I resent Dad being there too; it isn't easy to answer from this distance. Elaine and I did need to spread our wings more than in the past, and now we were back to travelling with our Father when it would have been more fun with our friends. Having said that I think the answer is probably no. Dad took his piano accordion, made it known that he could provide music for our early morning devotions in the open air and, loving performing as he did, probably played it at the concert. He led a study group each time, became affectionately known as Uncle Alf and blended in very well.

Though I did feel sorry for Mum being abandoned two long weekends a year, it wasn't a bad thing to be known as Uncle Alf's daughter.

Easter 1948 saw us off to Camp again, the fourth for Elaine and I, this time to be held at Young again. By this time we knew a number who came regularly, among them Ken Ward who has remained a lifelong friend.

Not long after returning home a letter addressed to me and postmarked Canberra arrived in the mail, signed Clyde Denton. Don't ask me what it said, but anyway we started writing to each other and very occasionally he would borrow his father's car and come to Merrilea for a weekend.

A group photo was always taken at these camps and when his first letter came, I had to go to mine, look hard and decide—yes, I *think* that one in the back row is Clyde, tall, dark, magnificent physique.

So we couldn't have seen much of each other; was it my glorious Titian hair or the fact that I was Uncle Alf's daughter that moved him to write to me?

We didn't get much time to ourselves. Elaine loved accompanying singers on the piano and Clyde liked singing so sometimes in the mornings that would be happening while I helped Mum with the necessary tasks. One memory from the mists of time was of him coming out of his room one morning and greeting me as I swept the hearth, by singing:

My love she looks so charming   *So early in the morning,*
She looks so sweet and charming   *In every high degree,*
She looks so sweet and charming   *So early in the morning,*
Sweeping away with a broom,   *Sweeping away with a broom*
She stole my heart away.

Wasn't that nice and romantic.

Perhaps my family more or less took over. There is a photo of us lined up beside our car, all dressed up: Mum, Dad, Elaine and I, and Clyde carrying a waterbag! Where on earth were we going that we needed that?

Dates with Clyde often included the family.

In 1950, he was selected to be one of a group to go to the Northern Territory and Kimberley areas to be involved in mapping. He was away five or more months and while we continued writing, friends from his church wrote him too, naturally and included one girl "M." whose letters came to mean more to him than mine. While still up north he wrote and broke off with me whatever our relationship may have been,

I wrote back saying '*Goodbye, Good luck and God bless. Beryl*'. I only saw him once more, when he told me that the girl "M." had called it off with him after a little while, and he expressed good wishes for my forthcoming marriage to George.

One visit Clyde brought a friend who had relations locally whom we knew.

The wife of one of the relations rang up to invite the two guys to their home for dinner the following evening. The next day she phoned again, rather flustered, and wondering if Elaine and I could come too! She hadn't included us before as she thought our parents wouldn't permit us to come.

I was 20, Elaine 22½. Can you believe it? Words fail me.

Katoomba Christian Convention

I think the first experience Elaine and I had of Katoomba Convention was Boxing Day 1950 till 3rd or 4th of January, 1951. Accommodation was in a big tent on the Convention grounds on Foster's Road, Echo Point, for members of the Crusader for Christ house party led by Alex Gilchrist.

I think our friend and neighbour, Peter Cramb, who owned a jazzy little red Singer, provided transport and was probably the person who told us about the Conventions. One free day he took us to Hawkesbury Agricultural College, where he had been a student, to visit a friend who had been his lecturer. At Katoomba morning, afternoon and evening there were meetings in the big marquee with wonderful singing and speakers, sometimes a missionary and once I noted in a letter home; a lecturer in archaeology. We were free to choose how many and which of these we went to, so we had free time to explore and enjoy the walks, waterfalls and beautiful scenery which was so close.

On New Year's Eve we all went up Katoomba Street where the usual celebrations would have been in progress, to join a crowd where there was a Christian open air witness by the Open Air Campaigners led by Ed Bentley. Time to walk home again and I was escorted by the most handsome young man I had ever put eyes on, 'tall, dark and handsome' as the saying goes. He was from New Zealand and his next stop was to be New Guinea. We walked back through a soft mountain mist, his arm around me; so-o-o romantic. (Sigh.)

The next year we were back again, this time with some more friends: Stella and Marj. Pfeiffer, Brenda Miller, Helen I'Anson and boyfriend Barry Holland, and his brother Maurice, not to mention George Walker who was on the scene by then.

Stopping at Bathurst on our way to Katoomba
Convention.

In a letter to Mum I mentioned that I had received a surprise
when on arrival I learned my name was on a list of those who had
permanent duties and had the rank of sergeant! *"I have to help serve
the meals each day; but it's not quite as bad as it sounds as I miss out on
all the vegetable peeling, washing up, waiting etc."*

One outing I remember was to Jenolan Caves; some of us
went shopping in the morning for things to make a picnic lunch
which we enjoyed beside the Cox River. We had enough for tea
too at the same place on the way home. We were joined by two
compatible Sydneyites, Grace Hunter and Ted Brown, making a
party of twelve. Grace was a dressmaking teacher and next year
she was appointed to Grenfell where Elaine and I were going to
tech. And in due course she cut out my wedding dress.

My Driving Lesson

1946-7: I don't know if it was my idea or Dad's that I should
learn to drive but one day he backed the car out of the garage

into a paddock where there was nothing but space; gave me a few instructions relating to letting the clutch out SLOWLY and pressing the accelerator GENTLY which I tried to follow but the car gave several startled leaps and stalled. I tried again with the same result. I then copped a lecture on the mechanics of cars and how the gears would be stripped or something I still don't understand.

The driving lesson given by my Dad when I was in my teens was not quite my last attempt to take steps that would hopefully lead to me having a driver's licence.

I married in October 1953 and by October 1964 had six gorgeous children, Alison, who was 10 years old, David—eight years, Glynis and Murray—four years, Kathryn—two years, and our new baby Jeanette. Six good reasons why driving lessons from George had not been on the agenda and probably wouldn't be for quite some time.

However, early in 1973 I did get a learner's permit and started lessons, but fate in the shape of severe drought intervened. It was one of the worst droughts ever in our local area but 50 kilometres away in the Cowra district, they were having a lush season. George sold our fifty cattle and drove 2200 sheep to his brother's farm at Wattamondara. Four hundred of these were sold at Cowra and three weeks later George drove the rest to "Pine Mount" north east of Cowra for seven weeks on agistment. Then George and David, who would have been enjoying May school holidays, with the loan of our friends Ken and Margaret Whiteman's caravan, took to the roads again for a month, bringing the sheep home the long way round so that they could be shorn in June.

All this disruption meant I didn't have a licenced driver available to continue learning and the three months allowed for the learner's permit expired. I did not bother to get another. Some people do give up easily don't they!

Elaine's Driver's Licence

At some time, I don't remember just when, Dad taught Elaine to drive and she obtained her driver's licence. I think one had to be 18 then. Dad went over to Temora and bought her a little blue two-seater Citroen. Aunty Dot said she remembered it being driven along the Temora streets with airmen hanging all over it, so it probably had quite a history.

Elaine with her first car.

Elaine used it to go to Greenethorpe where she had a few piano students. She would stay overnight with Uncle Selby and Aunty Clyda whose company she enjoyed, but they left Greenethorpe at the beginning of 1949.

We have a photo of her standing near the car with almond blossoms behind, taken in Spring 1947.

Twice in 1950, Elaine and I drove into Grenfell in the little blue car to watch the Grenfell Rugby League team play for the hotly contested Maher Cup which we had retained for four matches. For about 50 years the Cup had drawn large crowds to matches in RL Group 9 which covered towns from Cowra to Tumut, Cootamundra and Barmedman. Grenfell only won the coveted trophy twice more, on 13th and 30th September, 1952. In a letter to George on 17th September, 1952, I wrote:

"Have you heard the great news? Grenfell won the Maher Cup last Saturday! No doubt it was an occasion of great rejoicing as Gundagai have held it against all comers all the winter, but we showed 'em. I remember when we won the battered old cup last time, the Town Band marched to meet the homecoming heroes and there were great celebrations, champagne all round—I wonder if it was the same this time?"

Aunt Annie's Visit

There was great excitement in July, 1947 when we had a visit from Mum's Aunt Annie, her father's sister, from Glen Aplin near Stanthorpe in southeast Queensland. She was a lovely lady, another of the athletic Kings in her younger days. I learned later that she had quite a reputation as a painter on tin and that the Temora Museum had some of her works. We saw them there while on a visit a few years ago, and amazingly I have one too. I saw it when taking care of the things in Aunty Dot's house after her death and knew straight away what it was, so brought it home complete with its nail to poke into a crack in the wall and thereby hang it up.

Holidays with our Cousins the Grays

From time to time Elaine and I would have a few days with our cousins Edith, Joyce and Betty Gray; Ken was probably too young to participate. We used to sleep three to a double bed and in the morning were expected and encouraged to help a bit with chores—perhaps make some cookies—and then our time was our own, and we used to spend hours singing around the piano.

Elaine loved nothing better than accompanying singers and we attempted things such as Purcell's *Nymphs and Shepherds*, Handel's *Where'er You Walk*, Schubert's *To Music* as well as some lighter pieces, such as *Some Folk* by Stephen Foster (two-part harmony), and really doing them very well. Betty developed a truly glorious voice, and it was a joy to listen to her.

Narooma Holiday—1948

We had become very friendly with Len and Jess Kendall during the war years, mainly because of our musical involvements. She was a gentle, motherly lady and he was a brilliant violinist and very outgoing; a real livewire. They owned the local picture theatre, the Royal.

Other good friends were Don and Grace Cramb and their son Peter. Mum had become friends with Mrs Cramb when making camouflage nets early in the war and their friendships continued all their lives. We became neighbours when Dad bought Cumnock Farm in 1953. They had been having holidays at Narooma for years and started telling us we should really try to take one too. The Crambs used to stay at a guest house but had changed to camping because of the freedom. They, especially Mrs Cramb, loved fishing and didn't want to have to leave when the fish were biting, to come in for a meal.

Anyway, a camping holiday wasn't beyond our means so in 1948 the excitement and preparation began. That included doing cooking, making ginger nuts to eat when travelling—always a Pereira tradition to help ward off travel sickness—also a big sultana and light fruit cake, for morning or afternoon tea when Mum, ever hospitable, asked someone for a visit, as well as for ourselves.

Of course we went to church on the first Sunday there and virtue had its own reward as the organist Mrs Wilcox invited us out to her farm where blackberries grew—not the smallish fruit and hard to get at, smothered in weeds where one expects to meet a black snake any minute variety, but plants that had been imported from England by one of her husband's ancestors and were grown in a paddock that looked like a lawn, producing large luscious berries.

We were invited to pick as many as we liked, and on subsequent holidays they were one of the highlights. We liked them best washed, sprinkled with sugar and eaten with ice-cream. Part of being on holidays is having a change of diet and we really enjoyed the fish meals and a bread new to us, Promax.

We were soon part of the social life of camping and would go in groups to other places for a day's outing at a beach. Two other families joined our group, the Burgess family and the Cleavers. The latter lived in Canberra where they ran a taxi service, and insisted we spend a night with them on our way home. They were kindness itself. Mrs Cleaver gave us a comprehensive tour of the city and Mum, who was prone to get nervous in a car, especially if she thought it might go faster than 30 MPH (45km/h), trusted her completely, relaxed and thoroughly enjoyed herself. The Kendalls retired to Narooma and after that we were able to go up to their home on Tilba St and make jam from the berries to take home with us.

Next time we went the Burgess and Cleaver families weren't camping but we met the Jacksons from Brighton-le-sands and "clicked" with them straight away. They had a daughter Joan who was older than us and stayed at home, probably working, and a son John, who was younger. Mr Jackson helped Elaine with swimming lessons, those who liked it went fishing, but Fosters Bay was what suited us; one could hire a boat or just stand in the shallow water with a hand line and wait for a fish to come along and take the bait. I did some of that.

Altogether we had three such holidays at Narooma (1948, '49, and '50) at that time, all enjoyable with our friends. There were outings to other places—Tuross Lakes, Dalmeny, Bermagui, Mystery Bay and so on, and of course, blackberrying, fishing, and fun in the water. We have very fond memories of Narooma.

In February 1956 we had another holiday at Narooma, renting a unit in the Foster Bay area; leaving our daughter Alison with Grandma Walker and being joined by Mum, Dad and Elaine. Mum noted in her diary that in 12 days we had 14 inches of rain and that I had a nice hot meal and blackberries ready for them when they arrived. We had more trips, to Dalmeny and Bermagui, where Mr and Mrs Kendall, and Mrs Cramb and some of her family joined us for a picnic lunch and we went in the surf and had fun in the afternoon. One afternoon Dad, George and I went out on a boat on the Bay and caught some fish—records say I caught the most, 18. Elaine had at least one afternoon in the surf.

We had a lovely evening at the home of Mr and Mrs Kendall. It was great to hear Mr Kendall playing his violin again, and Elaine and I played two piano duets, movements from Beethoven symphonies. We made a second trip to Wilcox's for more blackberries and more jam making. Despite the weather not being ideal for holidays, we had a very good time.

Birthdays

As far as I can recall, birthdays were celebrated with family—perhaps the family from Spring Vale, or Uncle Arthur and Aunty Betty and family. There would always be an iced cake, and raspberry cordial to drink. To make this drink one bought small bottles of concentrate, Burnett's I think, and added it to a syrup of water and sugar, proportions given on the bottle. An inch or a little more in a glass of cool water made an enjoyable drink.

My birthday being in February, Mum was always doing well to get a couple of jellies to set in the cool safe. Elaine and I each celebrated our 21st's with a big do—a party to which all and sundry were invited. Mum made the fruit cake and Uncle Frank iced and decorated it.

Elaine's 21st Birthday Party

Elaine's party was on the actual day, the 7th August, 1947, and held in Spring Vale woolshed.

There would have been well over one hundred guests and we have lists of the songs for community singing, items given by people, games to be played, who 'spoke a few words' and who supported him or her, also lists of gifts and givers. The evening ended with cutting of the cake—a two-tiered fruit cake made by me (very successfully even if I say so myself) and iced and decorated by Uncle Frank Gray, this being followed by a sumptuous supper.

My 21st Birthday Party

There is a lengthy report of my 21st birthday party in a copy we have of *The Grenfell Record* dated 13th April, 1950. According to that report the party was held on Saturday, 25th March, as we were on holiday in Narooma for my actual birthday, 7th February. The delay was probably a good idea; we had a nice holiday with our friends, and a party with 100 people in a tin shearing shed during summer would have been rather hot and smelly.

It was a replica of Elaine's in many ways: held in Spring Vale woolshed; community singing, musical programme, games, supper, cutting the cake which had two tiers made by my mother and iced and decorated by Uncle Frank in cream with blue touches; speeches by Rev. Collard and Ron Diprose to which the guest of honour responded in a *"very appropriate and charming speech"*.

My gift from my parents was a lovely gold watch chosen by me, the first I had ever owned.

Holiday with Auntie Eva and Uncle Harrie— May 1949

Elaine and I received numerous invitations from Aunty Eva and Uncle Harrie to come to Sydney and have a holiday with them. In May 1949, the opportunity came to go back with them after they had been staying in Young. Off we went, full of excitement and anticipation at the thought of the "Big Smoke". Fortunately for us, Uncle Selby was there on a business trip and when that was completed, one morning he devoted himself to giving his two nieces a super treat. I will quote Elaine's letter home:

"We had fish for dinner at a very nice cafe opposite Hyde Park. Then we went and found the Conservatorium of Music, which is lovely. We found Miss Procter's friend and Beryl got her certificate which is to be posted home. She sent us to Frank Hutchins to see about the program and he is lovely. He looks just like a musician should look and was so kind and helpful. The man Beryl was to see about analysing her pieces had gone out so Beryl left her book with Miss Procter's friend and she is going to see him. After that we went for a trip over to Manly and I am sure you can imagine how I enjoyed it. It was absolutely lovely. I think Manly is a lovely place, I like it best of the suburbs I have seen. We went into a cafe and had special waffles with ice cream and strawberries and cream then came back and went and saw the pictures 'The Red Shoes'. It is the one Miss Procter recommended and we enjoyed it. There was a complete ballet in the picture and I enjoyed the dancing especially. When it was finished we had supper and came home after a wonderful day. We are very grateful to Uncle Selby for giving us such a good day."

In a letter contained in the same envelope I wrote: *"Apart from the day with Uncle Selby, things have been very quiet; the most exciting things I have done are wash up—five a day—and peel potatoes. I would like to have had a couple of outings in town but I don't think anyone here is likely to take us. Aunty Eva has been tired. Elaine is a surprise, she adored the crowds, electric trains and general hustle and bustle. She is firmly convinced she could find her way around quite well but I'm not so keen."*

After a few more days there, Aunty Stella came and helped us with our baggage to Rockdale where she and Uncle Bob lived. I wrote, *"I'm not sure how we are spending the rest of the time but we are sure to have a lovely time. Aunty Stella says we won't do any work now, and she will get a pick and shovel and a couple of Council men to clean out the dirt when we are gone."*

Elaine's letter: *"We are having a lovely time here. On Saturday Aunty Stella took us for a lovely walk along the beach and we had tea and the evening with the Jackson's. On Sunday afternoon Mr J. took us for a (words fail me to describe it) drive over most of Sydney and all the eastern beaches. On Sunday night we went to church at the Lyceum and enjoyed it very much. This afternoon we are going to the city, and then Aunty Stella is taking us to her friend Maud Watkins for tea."* This was the last letter before going home by train on the 1st April.

Dear Aunty Stella, I can see the twinkle in her eye when she spoke of getting the Council men in. It was her way of saying: "No chores, you're here to have a good time and see new things".

I remember Mum saying that Aunty Stella had often said when we were kiddies that she would love to have us down there and show us the sights, especially the shop's displays at Christmas time, but that didn't ever happen. She had no children of her own and possessed a big, generous heart.

Margaret Hughes & Alex Anderson Wedding— 26th May, 1951

We all received invitations to the marriage of Mum's best friend, Nell Hughes's daughter Margaret's wedding but for some reason Mum, Dad and Elaine were unable to be there so it was up to me to represent the family. The wedding was held at Central Baptist Church, George Street, Sydney.

I wrote letters home so I have a reasonably good record of what I did after the wedding but really next to no information about the wedding itself. Mum kept two envelopes labelled 1 & 2 and 3 & 4, but one has gone astray. I think the best I can do is quote my letters.

Thursday 24th May: *"Dearest Family, Well I suppose you are wondering what sort of trip I had and how things are. Had a good trip although I only had about three hours sleep, the train was rather rough and noisy. We arrived about 25 minutes late, Uncle Clarrie went with me to the entrance to the electric trains and then I went all by myself down the passages and stairs and found the right platform and right train. Wasn't I clever? Aunty Stella was at Kogarah to meet me, and our tongues haven't stop wagging yet. I rang Margaret and had a nice talk and I'm going in to help decorate the church between 10 and 10.30 Saturday morning. Mrs Hughes is going to get dressed for the wedding at the church buildings and I think I will do the same. Margaret had a lovely time at the social and received some lovely gifts, among them Bon Ami and sandsoap for her and Rennies and Aspros for Alex.*

"I bought a Herald this morning and we have been looking up all the things we want to see. I will write again soon, and don't worry, I'm going to have a gay time. See that Barney is a good boy and doesn't fight Benjy."

Second letter dated Monday, 28th May: *"We met Aunty Al and Estelle Friday Morning and had the morning looking at shops and after lunch they went home and Aunty Stella and I went to Everyman's Centre and saw Alex Gilchrist. We then went around to Palings buildings and met Miss Morton and she gave us a voucher for three things. We are going to hear Justin Bonn, a Dutch tenor at the Conservatorium tonight, to the Royal Theatre to see Worm's Eye View with Gordon Chater on Thursday night and today week I am going to the Town Hall to hear Yehudi Menuhin. Aunty Stell says she's not talking to him since he had his divorce. We are also hoping to see the Ballet and the Ice Follies. Our trouble is to know how to fit everything in. We have been laughing over the Star Guide in yesterday's Telegraph. Aunty Stella's says 'Why not take a few days off and have some fun? Some of you have been driving yourselves very hard. Join a group and extend or accept invitations. Relax on Friday and get a new lease of life.' Mine says 'Stepping out? That's the password this week. Many of you will find yourselves entangled in a maze of social activities with interesting contacts.' The wedding was lovely and I enjoyed helping decorate the church; I'll tell you all about it when I see you. I have promised to have a day with Mrs Hughes.*

"I'm getting very clever at finding my way around. After the wedding, I found my way back to Central and went out to Coral's place and then on out to Parramatta Town Hall to the 'This is Life Rally'. Then I had the night at Coral's place and Sunday morning, Mrs Davis and I went to church and who was there to conduct the service but Don Renolds. He is as nice and even nicer than ever Elaine. As they had no one to conduct the 'big' Sunday School, he stayed on and did that for them and I played the organ and took a class. Then we went round to North Auburn to a Fellowship tea. I was fortunate enough to get a lift back with some of the church folk to Auburn Station and arrived back at Aunty Stella's before eight."

I have left out comments on the weather, names of people I met and other bits of trivia. Uncle Bob worked with trains and played with trains all his spare time and had a top class set up of model electric trains in his garage. I was given a comprehensive demonstration, also taken to the pictures to see Spencer Tracy in North West Passage before leaving for home by train on the seventh of June.

Last letter dated 3rd June:

"We thoroughly enjoyed Worm's Eye View. Aunt Stell says she can't remember when she laughed so much, and it really was entertaining. I wish I could pick you three up and send you down there to see it. It ran for three years in London.

"*I had Thursday at Aunty Eva's and went for lunch and then we had a lovely talk. I had tea there and then went on into town and met Aunty Stella at Central and we went to the theatre together.*

"*Friday we met Aunty Al and Estelle and had lunch with 'Ma' (Aunty Stell's mother in law). Then I booked a seat for the ballet Tuesday night. I'll be seeing 'Les Sylphides', 'The Black Swan', and 'Petrouchka'.*

"*Then at four Aunty Stell and I went to Rozelle and had tea with Al, Clarrie and Marie, then at seven Marie and I caught a bus back into town and went to the Jungle Doctor Rally at the Assembly Hall in Margaret Street. Nancy Watts and John Edwards were waiting on the steps for us and we all sat together. Dr Paul White compered it himself, we sang, saw lovely Kodachrome films of Africa, met a missionary just returned from Dr White's hospital, a teacher and two nursing sisters and all round we had a lovely time, so glad we were there.*

"*Yesterday Jacksons called for me at 10am and we went to the Sydney Cricket Ground to see the Frenchmen play Sydney football; it was 19 points each and was very exciting. Then we had tea with them and they drove me into town where I went to the Youth Rally at Everyman's Centre, the faithful John and Nancy were there. I enjoyed myself.*

"*This afternoon we are going into the Town Hall to the Grand Organ and Military band recital. Florence Taylor is going to be soloist and I'm looking forward to it.*"

I added a postscript saying: "*I will enclose the programme from this afternoon's (free!) concert. It was lovely.*"

The programme is in the envelope with the letter; unfortunately all the others I may have had have disappeared over the years. As you can see I had a great time; the Dutch tenor sang a lot of Schuman, just my cup of tea, and seeing live ballet for the first time was breathtaking—and of course Yehudi Menuhin was wonderful. Lucky me to have the opportunity.

P.S. The bride wore white satin.

★★★★

There was always a cat: Breow—the last.

A quotation from a book describing the Turkish Van breed of cats: *A loving cat, it eagerly spreads its affection throughout the family but gives it most to a chosen individual.* That was our Breow.

I heard about Breow—called Browser—before I ever met him. He lived with his owner in East Street. My sister used to visit a friend nearby and had met him as he had a reputation for going around the neighbours and saying hello.'

She told me about this magnificent cat, saying he was a Turkish Van. He certainly met all the book's criteria: *The body is long but sturdy with tail and legs of medium length, muscular of shoulders and neck. The head should be shaped like a short wedge, with well feathered, large, upright ears and a long nose. The fur should be long, soft and silky to the roots with a woolly undercoat and a full tail. The main colour should be chalk white, but with auburn markings, an auburn tail with fainter auburn rings.* He was all of that plus a very impressive ruff, especially in winter.

Breow.

115

My first encounters with him were in 1997. He had moved with his owners into Dagmar Street opposite Elaine's home. She was ill with cancer and each night I went up and settled her for the night then walked home. Breow would always be waiting about 9 o'çlock each night to escort me home. One day he jumped over the fence looking very pleased with himself and I squirted water at him from the hose as I didn't really want to steal someone else's cat.

Another time Norma brought us a box of meat from the farm and Breow arrived about two minutes later, telling me he was starving. What could I do but give him some?

Carolyn, his owner, said to me once; "don't give him anything to eat or you will never get rid of him!" She had a business, two little children, a dog and a husband who wasn't fond of cats, so probably Breow was not getting the kind of lifestyle and attention he felt he deserved.

Perhaps he had also heard the quotation from a book I have: *A cat's affinity has to be won. Unlike a dog, it won't remain with an inferior owner out of a misdirected sense of devotion. However, a cat will recognise a good owner and respond with affection and companionship.* Did he ever!

By mid-1999, Breow was stepping up his campaign to come and live with us. He would appear in the garden or at the door. I would ask: "And what is your name?" He would always look up at me and say: "Breow," rolling the sound from 'b' to 'r' making almost a purring sound. So, I capitulated, he could and did make his home with us, with the name of Breow.

He was not a cat who jumped onto people's laps but from time to time, I would pick him up, sit him on my lap and pet and stroke him, but after a few minutes he would say: "that was very nice, but I'm getting down now" and would proceed to do so. He used to sleep on the foot of our bed with his own bedding (some pieces of old sheets) and being a queen-sized bed there was plenty of room for three.

One of the things we enjoyed was the welcome home—even if only after an evening out. As we turned into our laneway, we would see him trot across to the back gate or sit in the roadway, his eyes shining in the headlight beam—he was always there. Although it is now three years since he died we still both miss those shining eyes when we turn into the lane at night.

I particularly remember one reunion which was after we had enjoyed a five day trip to Wentworth with Probus in early May 2010. I had asked Kathy Taylor to look after him and had made up little parcels of chicken and steaks strips to be fed to him as well as tinned and dry food. She would shut him in the laundry at night where his toilet tray was, also water and chair with a cushion for his comfort, then let him out again in the morning. She loved cats and was happy to do this for us but he must have missed us because I received a welcome home such as I had never before experienced.

He wasn't on the scene when we arrived home so I went to the back gate and called him. He came, positively galloping down the lane from Forbes St., calling "OH, OOOHH", and leapt up into my arms! My diary for that day included *"much purring from us both"*.

However, things were changing and we had had a couple of trips to the vet at Young and learnt that his kidneys weren't functioning properly and on Monday, 5th July 2010, I noted in my diary: *"Breow is changing, he put himself on my lap for the first time ever and is still not eating so much."* The next three nights I noted that he sat on my lap.

From then on it was just a matter of feeding him whatever kept him happy, which was being given all the breast meat from the chickens we bought at IGA and being allowed to sit on my lap in the evenings hour after hour.

The poor darling was wanting his "Mum" and couldn't get close enough, even climbing up on my bosom right under my chin. I would postpone going to bed as long as I could but eventually I had to make the effort to lift him up and get myself out of the chair. And a big effort was needed too, with Breow sitting on my chest and hanging on with both paws, replacing them as fast as I disengaged them. He just didn't want to part with his mum.

His breath was awful, and George and I had fears he might get away from us and die elsewhere. He was much frailer so on 6th September, George rang Chris, our local vet and he agreed to come down and "put Breow to sleep" at 10am that morning.

Breow and I had another good half hour back in our chair where we had spent so many hours recently, before I had to say "Goodbye". We wrapped him in his loved blankets he slept on and buried him, too, in the Arboretum.

There will never be another Breow.

★★★★

The Beryl and George Story Begins
22nd March, 1951

Easter came a little earlier that year; from Thursday, 22nd March to Monday 26th; and we attended the Crusader Camp held at Canberra Methodist Church.

There was a big group of us and as always a really good time was enjoyed, and then it was time for goodbyes. There were no stand out moments for me.

But some 25 miles (36 kilometres) approximately away, a young man was from time to time doing some hard thinking. March passed.

"Will I or wont I? She is Uncle Alf's daughter, has a farming background, the same religion. That's three pluses." April came and went.

More deliberation. The dictionary defines that as "careful consideration, discussion, debate, care, avoidance of precipitancy, slowness of movement". Spot on!

"I do want to find a wife; but she is a redhead! Some say they have a terrible temper!" May came and went.

Still more deliberation. *"Mum says 'faint heart never won fair lady'."* Desperation conquered and on 3rd June he sat down and wrote a letter to me. It contained the obligatory comments on the weather, also the church news, the Order of Knights, the new minister and then asking me to let him know when the Christian Endeavour meetings were held in Grenfell. Finished up with *I* am not making any promises mind you and if I don't manage to get to a C.E. Meeting will probably see you at the next Crusader Camp." Signed, *Yours in Christian friendship, George Walker.* The next camp wouldn't be until next October!

Hardly the approach to sweep a girl off her feet but ….

I had been in Sydney attending my good friend Margaret Hughes's wedding followed by a holiday and returned on Friday, 9th June. I wrote a reply three days later with the required information, adding an invitation to the evening meal with us if suitable and directions where to find Merrilea. Signed, *Yours in felawschippe, Beryl Pereira.* A song called *Lo, here is felawschippe* was the signature song of the Crusader movement.

George's diary 29th June, 1951: *"Margaret and I went to the Pereira's for tea then the meeting at Grenfell. Beryl, Elaine, Bruce Brown and Les Pfeiffer came in my Austin."* Did he really need to bring his sister for moral support?

On 15th July in his fourth letter George said: *"I think I ought to tell you something Beryl. I am wondering if I haven't been just a little bit deceitful. I have been quite sincere in my desire to attend the meetings in Grenfell but I think I have another motive as well—to see you. I do hope that I will not be any less welcome because of that but please be frank with me."* !!!??!!

The poor fellow—why would any girl think less of him for what he termed being a little bit deceitful? It would have been more flattering, naturally, if he had expressed interest in me in his first letter but of course I wasn't fooled, feminine instinct had taken care of that.

Although, while pondering whether it was my sparkling personality, glowing titian hair and musical talent or the fact that I was Uncle Alf's daughter, that sparked his interest, I reluctantly had to come to the conclusion it was the latter. Another identity crisis!!

George claims he helped me climb onto the back of a truck which was transporting a number of us to a service at Wattle

Park church where I was to be organist, but I don't remember it. Probably I was one of a number of girls.

George, the Junior Farmer Celebrity

I didn't have to look at a camp photograph as he was already known to me in a way as I had seen his photo in the Land Newspaper. He had been Junior Farmer Grand Champion of the Year in 1948 with his project being tree growing and later had the honour of addressing the Forestry Advisory Council of NSW and being presented with an Honorary Members badge, which he still sometimes wears. Miss Judith Cassell who, under the name of "Blue Gum" wrote a regular column on tree planting in the Land, described George's achievements in glowing terms. She even quoted at length his address to F.A.C.

And though he hadn't noticed me, we had previously been to one or two of the same camps; so I was interested to see it was a Christian who was making such a name for himself.

Courtship

In a letter from George dated Saturday, 21st July,1951: *"went over to Beryl's about 3.30. We talked together till tea, then had a game of billiards with Uncle Alf, a sing song and looked at snaps. Very enjoyable evening."*

So an exchange of letters took place, all bearing a 3½d stamp, together with visits when George could fit them in with his many commitments: church, OK's, Junior Farmer's, Sunday School at Wattamondara every Sunday at 2pm, sermon preparation and delivery, P&C secretary for Watta School, and Watta Bush Fire Brigade—many of these in an advisory or leadership role.

From early October we had been saying we must have a day or afternoon exploring the hills behind Merrilea and climbing the big rock; but it was not until 18th October that it happened. George wrote in his diary: *"I went over to Beryl's and we went for a hike to the BIG ROCK and had a picnic in the hills and had a lovely time together."*

Christmas 1951, George had dinner with his family then came to Spring Vale where the Pereira clan were gathered. He spent the night at Merrilea to be ready for a start next morning for the Katoomba Convention, travelling with the Pfeiffers, Helen I'Anson, Bruce Brown, Peter Cramb, Brenda Miller and of course Elaine and I. We had a picnic lunch in Bathurst Park on the way there.

Friday, 3rd January, I received my first proposal of marriage—a bit of a shock to me as George hadn't even plucked up the courage to kiss me and you do want to know you welcome a man's kisses before you commit yourself to marriage!

During courtship.

First Kiss

I wasn't at all discouraging though and things remained much as they were before and on the 24th February, seven and a half weeks later, **HE KISSED ME!**

The tempo of our romance accelerated and, when driving home after the Easter Crusader Camp at Batlow on Monday 14th April, 1952, we realised belatedly that we had not noticed the turn off to Cootamundra until we found ourselves at Jugiong— which was not where we were supposed to be. We were amused, rather than disconcerted, turned around, headed back the way we had come, not missing the turn off to from the highway to Cootamundra this time. We went to a cafe and while seated there, sharing a plate of toasted sandwiches, I felt an overflow of love and tenderness for George and knew my happiness would be in becoming his wife.

In a letter dated 16th April I said: *"Elaine says to tell you she still laughs every time she thinks of Jugiong and I must admit I have had many a smile over the whole affair too. What the rest of the crowd would have had to say had they only known; I can just imagine, too!"*

Sunday, 27th April: *"We wish Dot well with her cooking. As far as 'wanting to cook as well as Elaine and Beryl,' I don't know though! Still I could be worse I suppose; I can only remember having two flops in all the years I've been cooking so that's not a bad record. Incidentally they were both after Crusader Camps, so perhaps that explains them. One, I remember was a batch of small cakes in which I neglected to put the sugar!"*

Wednesday 11th June: In a postscript to a letter to George I said: *"You said in your last letter that you often tried to read between the lines in my letters to find out just what I really thought of you. Ask me sometime and I'll tell you."* That must have given him the needed push and 11 days later we were engaged!

It was more than two months after our Jugiong episode when, on 22nd June, George proposed and I said, "YES". This was after he had conducted a church service in Cowra, the subject being, "David slew the Philistine". Next morning he came into my bedroom with a cup of tea; still a wee bit shyly but looking very pleased with himself and his new status as my BETROTHED. George had told his Mum and she said she was not a bit surprised at the news.

After a while I packed up and George drove me home and we told my family our news at the dinner table. We remember Mum had a rather unexpected reaction—"ENGAGED!" as though it was a surprise for her; after all I *was* 23 years and 4 months old and we had been writing to and visiting each other for a year. George stayed that afternoon and evening and was soon back to reality. The first entry in his diary next day was: *Picked up wool from three dead sheep.*

In a letter to George dated 25th June, I said: "*Elaine is very funny; she is so excited that she says she shall 'burst' if she has to keep things a secret much longer;*" and is immensely gratified that I have all the symptoms of a person in love—pink cheeks, bright eyes, no appetite etc.

The Ring

We weren't making a public announcement until I was wearing the ring, and on the 1st of July we went to Young and looked at rings but weren't satisfied, so we drove to Sydney the next day and stayed with Aunty Eva and Uncle Harrie. The following day we went by train into the city and chose our ring at Bruce and Walsh. We then embarked on a hectic round of visiting every relation and friend we could manage. That very afternoon we had afternoon tea and the evening meal with Uncle Selby and Auntie Clyda, then across to Bankstown to see Aunty Laurel and Beryl.

The next morning we relaxed and, after lunch, drove to Waverley and spent an hour at Bondi until Margaret came from an exam at 3.30pm at Waverley Methodist War Memorial Hospital where she was nursing. We all went to Kogarah, called on the Bradshaw's and Aunty Stella, the Jacksons, and Aunty Margaret back at Bondi Junction and, after taking Margaret back to the Hospital, returned to Eastwood and bed at 11pm.

We left for home the next morning, 5th July, and had a leisurely trip. It started snowing at Katoomba—the country was white with snow for some distance through Lithgow, Bathurst, Blayney, Carcoar and Lyndhurst, and we enjoyed the unaccustomed and very beautiful scenery.

Home again, in a letter to George dated Wednesday 9th July I wrote: *"I have been terribly 'collar proud' since returning home; but will soon have to take my head out of the clouds and come back to earth. I'm still doing silly things too; I wonder how long that stage lasts? I collected my wits enough Sunday night to write and thank Eva and Harrie for having us, but I'm a terribly useless sort of person to have around the place. I just wander 'round aimlessly all the time, out in the garden for a while, back inside where I start doing something then leave it halfway through to go and have a look at some things in my chest of drawers, back to the sunshine then inside again to have another look at my ring and so on—really this will have to end!"*

It is time to give dear Barney a mention too; in the same letter I wrote: *"Poor old Barney has been almost pathetic in his happiness at having me home again, is very 'purry' and sticks closer than a brother; even preferring my knee to the rocking chair. So what more need I say?"*

Excerpts from my letters to George

Tuesday, 22nd January 1952: *"By the way all the attention these kittens received Saturday and Sunday very nearly ruined them. Monday morning I woke up at six to find that the two of them had clawed open the gauze of my window at one end and one was seated in the window and the other comfortably curled up on the spare bed! Weren't they brats?"*

Tuesday, 25th January: *"Barney has just arrived home looking very hot so I gave him a saucer of cold egg nog from the frig. This morning we were all having one and he asked for his share; which he was given, and which he certainly appreciated. What a cat is mine!"*

Sunday, 3rd February: *"Mr and Mrs Cramb and Peter came out last night and had tea and evening with us. I did so wish you could have been with us and met them and heard all about their trip on the Continent, England and Scotland. It was so wonderfully interesting and Mrs Cramb didn't stop talking about it all from the time they arrived till they left near midnight. Mother always says she is as good as a tonic to one; and she really is too, so cheery and original. Mr Cramb is a particularly nice person too. He doesn't get a chance to say much but sits and smiles lovingly at her."*

Monday, 15th February: *"Barney and I are having a lovely time together with ripe grapes now, he is just crazy about them. The birdies are too but Dad and I have lessened their numbers somewhat and disturbed their peace, so they aren't having it all their own way."*

Wednesday, 24th February: *"By the way; if you happen to be near the Lost Property Office any time between now and Saturday, would you call in and make enquiries about my straw hat with the rose on it. I realised this morning that I had left it in your car. Tell Stan I know feed is scarce but he is not to feed it to the cow!"*

Tuesday, 11th March—Beginning dressmaking lessons
"This is a surprise—I decided all of a sudden on Sunday to learn dressmaking and went in to Grenfell with Beth and Shirley Clements yesterday for my first lesson. I have always loudly maintained that I loathed sewing in any shape or form, but I decided it would be foolish not to take my chance and will probably quite like it if I get on well. I'm determined to grit my teeth and stick it out for a year at least. I am sorry

*I will have miss some lessons while I am away; particularly as I've missed
two already; but still I need a holiday."*

It is no wonder I didn't like sewing. A couple of times during
Primary School, we had a sewing teacher for a few weeks and all I
had to show for it was one white pillowslip, the top hem laboriously
hand sewn with tiny stitches by me—talk about *boring* and the
other achievement was a very small square of white material, the
hem again hand stitched with a little piece of lace across one corner
with a wobbly G stitched inside it in mauve fancywork silk, and
a handkerchief, rather grubby from my hot little hands which
probably didn't get washed overmuch when at school. Both of
these were offerings for my mother, and neither have been used.
They were kept and are here among other things I inherited.

I continued with lessons at Tech, Elaine and I going to
Greenethorpe that year and Grenfell in 1953 when Grace Hunter,
whom we had met at Katoomba, became our teacher. Despite
having less than two years' tuition, what I learned was very useful
in the years ahead. Apart from blouses which I don't remember and
two dresses which I do, most of my sewing had been lingerie. The
floral pink satin dressing gown tried my patience sorely, also sets
of slips, panties, nightgowns, in one case with matching bedjacket.
All of these, while quite glamorous, weren't very practical.

By mid-March 1954, I was married, visiting at Cumnock
Farm, buying material and, with Elaine and Mum's help, making
nightdresses for the coming baby. In a letter to George I wrote: *"I
bought half a dozen singlets at Mrs Alf Stiff's baby wear shop at four and
sixpence each, one dozen nappies—3 pounds 6 shillings; isn't it awful but
they are things we need to have. We, bought some nice material for warm
nighties at Mrs Goulder's, and yesterday cut out four and commenced
sewing them; we can make them for less than half the cost of the cheapest
readymade ones.*

*Darling, your letters still affect me the way they used to before we were
married—after yours arrived I was most industriously pinning a sleeve into*

the armhole and when I had finally completed the job found that I had pinned the <u>wrist</u> to the armhole!"

I did a lot of sewing for my daughters as time went by, not that I did it for the fun of it but friends seemed to give me materials and then I had to do something with it. George's cousin, Roger Hewitt spent a school holiday with us once and as a 'thank you' Aunty Meg gave me a quantity of check material. I finally made it into three dresses—one each for Alison, Kathryn and Jeanette. Also my very good friend, Fay Wright gave me a couple of dresses she didn't wear and one was 'bubble' nylon that I made into dresses for Alison and Jeanette. I also made the girls' primary school uniforms and Alison's Brownie and Girl Guide uniforms. They have been simplified in recent times but back in the mid-sixties making them presented a really big challenge but a matching sense of achievement when the task was completed.

Letter to George, 11th March 1952: *"I've had a hectic week—this morning after an early start (8.30) I went through the house thoroughly with broom, mop and duster, then made five dozen jam drops for our holidays—they are lovely, too. This afternoon I was Daddy's helper; I was way down in the well with him shovelling buckets of wet mud, cement etc for Ernest to pull up and throw away. When I wasn't doing that I was chipping old cement off, and then after lunch Elaine joined me and we bailed out all the water that was left. Altogether I was down there 4½-5 hours, working hard all the time so you can well believe I am feeling rather tired tonight. We expect to be leaving on our holiday on Monday now but where to we haven't decided yet."*

Toowoon Bay Holiday

We left on our holiday at 11.45am, Monday, 17th March as planned and spent the night at Cedar Lodge Cabins at Mount Victoria; all of us enjoying the experience. Next morning we

were on our way again at 8.45am, Elaine and I making sure
Dad drove to Katoomba by way of the Cliff Drive and stopping
at Echo Point, which Mum and Dad loved. Then on again,
arriving at the Toowoon Bay camping ground at 5pm. We had
a really enjoyable time there; the camping ground was near the
surf, which we enjoyed. The beach was good for walks with
interesting rock pools, the only minus—no fishing for Dad who
had been looking forward to that. There were pleasant drives
not far away. We spent one day with our ex-Grenfellite friends
Don and Daisy Davies who had bought a dairy farm near
Wyong and they had one day with us. George joined us on 1st
April. The next day was cloudy but George fitted in a couple of
swims and we went for a drive to The Entrance. On 3rd April,
George and I went for a walk, those who swam had a swim
and then we packed up just before rain started and we went
to Don and Daisy's for the night. Heading for home the next
morning we had lunch with Aunty Al Litt at Wentworthville
and tea at Bathurst. George and I went on ahead arriving at
Merrilea at 9pm.

Letter to George, 18th November 1952: *"Uncle Claude at
Chellews Young showed me all the materials he had suitable for a wedding
dress. He didn't have anything special and says they are the lowest in that
line that they have ever been and have lost three wedding orders lately
because they haven't been able to get what was wanted. He added that
it was the worst possible time to be buying that type of thing; but hoping
things will be better when import restrictions are lifted in January. I have
done a couple of sketches of dresses and have almost decided on the style I
want; so there is that much progress to report anyway."*

Tuesday, 23rd December: *"Barney is sitting beside me beside
me being a big pest, wanting me to go out into the orchard with him
and feed him apricots which aren't yet ripe. I have promised to go with*

him when it is cool tonight, so he will have to be satisfied with that. He woke me up shortly after five yesterday morning; he had let himself into the dining room—the outside door wasn't clicked—with a baby rabbit, fortunately dead."

Cumnock Farm

At the beginning of December, 1952, my Dad bought Cumnock Farm: 552 acres, six miles from Grenfell on the Young Road for 31 pounds, 10 shillings ($63) an acre. On Sunday 20th November I wrote to George: *"Golly, I will be thankful when tomorrow is over—I hardly know what I hope will happen—there is so much 'for' and 'against' on both sides."*

Helen Price, Elaine and I (left) with our dog
Flapper's puppies at Merrilea.

Sunday 7th December: *"Well, here it is Sunday again; what a change in our lives this past week has brought about. Dad's cousin Thelma Fenton and her husband Allan paid us a surprise visit to congratulate us on getting the property and to say how glad they were. It was really lovely of them and we did appreciate it. Allan is an ex-banker and says we can't go wrong with it and wants to lend us his machinery and do anything to help he can."*

I remember Mum telling me he told her not to deny herself anything she needed or desired; the little amounts she might have spent would make no difference to the big picture.

In the same letter I wrote: *"Coming home from Young we called around at the new farm and had a look around. Not a door in the house was locked so we just walked in like that! There are a number of trees and a fairly large garden; grass is everywhere, feet high but we will get it in order in time. I think Dad intends to go out next Saturday afternoon and plant some tomatoes and get some sort of a garden started, pumpkins etc, so I guess he will want all hands and the cook to help."*

In her Journal my Mother wrote: *"On the fourteenth of January, 1953 we shifted out to Cumnock Farm. Alf bought it from Don Gibb at Auction sale on the 3rd December, 1952. He paid P31-14-0 an acre, a record up to that date in our area; 552 acres. Our first night here Alf sat down and played hymns on our organ; we were so happy to be here.*

"When Alf and I were married we went to live at Merrilea and we were there for 39½ years. We left it without any regrets although we had a very happy home there. Our two daughters Elaine and Beryl were born in Grenfell and grew up at Merrilea."

Dad often had his frustrations in his work situation. Although Merrilea was his, it was not his to use as he chose as it was treated as though it was part of Spring Vale and G.H.P. was the one who made the decisions. There was not a lot of farming country and G.H.P. had a fear of being caught overstocked if a drought came; as a consequence, the flock of sheep was not as big as it could and should have been; therefore not a lot of money for three family units.

In 1939, Dad and Uncle Arthur took the lorry and shifted Uncle Selby and Aunty Clyda's possessions from Gunnedah, where he had worked as an insurance agent, to Greenethorpe where he was to be a Stock and Station agent.

I don't know how long afterwards Dad mentioned to his father how he liked the look of some of the land he had seen around Gunnedah and was told: *"If you leave here you won't get a penny from me!"*

So that was the way it remained through war years and drought, but Dad didn't forget his need and ambition to be his own man, and when Cumnock Farm was advertised for sale, Dad was determined to buy it no matter what it cost.

The losing bidder at the auction had a father who was a doctor in Sydney, so probably there was money behind him, but I'm confident there would have been many prayers ascending to heaven from my parents.

Dad owned the block of land opposite the Cowra Road Methodist Church (the little blue church today) and sold it to his brother Arthur. The main block of Merrilea was sold to our next door neighbour, Mr Cobham.

I remember one time when I was probably in my mid-teens, driving with Dad to Young via the Grenfell to Young road. After passing Schneider's Lane and coming to the brow of the hill—the road way was higher then, above the present cutting—I was enthralled by the beauty of the scene to our right. I find it hard to find words to explain the effect it had on me but I feasted my eyes on it then—and I still do!

Was it a preview of the Promised Land? Maybe, because in time almost all I was looking at that day became our family's. Firstly Cumnock Farm, bought by my father in December, 1952; 552 acres at P31-14-0 ($63.40). George and I obtained 437 acres on Rumbles Lane in June 1960 at P27-10-0. On 27th March, 1976, we bought 1049 acres of 'Weddin View' adjoining the northern boundary of Cumnock Farm and going to Schneider's

Lane. The price was \$120 an acre, a total of \$125,716.30 and it was bought in our son David's name.

About 1997, a block of 187 acres which intruded between Cumnock Farm and 'Rumbles' was bought in our son Murray's name for a total of \$100,000.

Over the years numerous people have commented on the beauty of this stretch of land which so excited my senses all those years ago. In 2012 it is farmed very well by David and Murray, and with thousands of trees planted on it, it looks better than ever.

Preparing to move

Letter to George, Friday 26th December 1952: *"I don't suppose I will be writing this address at the top of my page very many more times. We began the packing today, empty jars, preserves, some rarely used kitchen utensils, etc. Arthur Parker proved a very handy person at wrapping and packing jars and so on. It will be an almighty task but it is good to have made a start.*

"The rain has put a stop to the stripping, so we will perhaps be going out to the farm all day and make a start on the garden and cleaning up operations. Dad wants to have another look at the paddocks and decide where to put his sheep which he will take delivery of tomorrow week. So it looks as though we will be having an all day picnic or, as Uncle Arthur says, 'a garden fete and all bring your own tools!'

"We had a snifter of a storm about six, Uncle Arthur was under the kitchen table; it wasn't quite that bad but the thunder was very loud and none of us enjoyed it. We had 50 points of rain in that storm and more since."

P.S. Written Sunday 28th December: *"I have two messages for you, Dot says to tell you they fell in love with Cumnock Farm and Arthur says he wished you were with us for the garden party! We went out shortly after 11 o'clock and didn't do a great deal as it was terribly hot and steamy but we planted some tomatoes, beans and marrow seeds and*

Dad went around his fences. Ruby, Claude and Mavis came out to see us in the afternoon.

"11pm: Our family has increased by two—no, not puppies or kittens; John Jackson and his friend Alan arrived unexpectedly."

Tuesday 30th December: *"I think Dad will probably be taking Dot and Arthur home to Temora this weekend, they will have had a nice length visit by then and have been a big help to us. John and Alan had to leave us today; they didn't want to but Alan has to start work again Thursday."*

Letter to George, Tuesday, 30th December 1952: *"This morning I was awakened to find Elaine bending over me saying, 'Wake up Beryl, someone wants you'. Naturally enough I wanted to know who it was and was told it was Mr. Quarmby's cat! I was only half awake and wondered if I was mad or hearing right; but it was only too true. Quarmby's are going on a holiday, and unable to take their kitty and after the Quarterly Meeting last night, asked Dad if he would take the kitten home for ME to look after!*

"Poor Kitty Quarmby, she is terribly frightened of the other cats and as the house is full of rowdy people, she is not going to have an easy time getting 'rehabilitated', but at present is curled up in the rocking chair, quite happily and has been having a game with Dad. We have kept her inside most of the day; I hate to think what might happen to her if she met the puppies; they are real heathens. So you can see we will have a real responsibility for the next two or three or whatever it is, weeks. Today she has taken more of my time than a baby would, but I hope we will soon get used to each other."

Monday 5th January: *"I did some more sorting out and recycling in some drawers and boxes this afternoon and as a result another big bundle of junk was carted out to be burned but in spite of the wicked hint I gave you yesterday no blue envelopes and their contents from my beloved were included in that heap; that is not to be their fate.*

"Dad came home with three more aprons for me from Aunty Pearl. They are lovely ones, two 'sensible' and one 'silly frilly'. I didn't expect her to make them up; she was only supposed to cut them out but it was sweet of her and I must write and thank her."

Thursday 8th January 1953: "Guess what? Kitty Quarmby will actually PURR for me now! I was beginning to think she couldn't. She is dear little pussy and very good; poor thing, I don't think she will appreciate the second move but that can't be helped.

"Well darling, I guess this is the last time I will be writing you a letter from Merrilea. We have been flat out all the week packing and are all beginning to feel very tired. The house looks simply terrible, boxes and cases heaped everywhere and all the pictures, books and ornaments packed away. Anyway, the back is well and truly broken of the first part of the business of moving and it will be all over and done within a few weeks' time, thank goodness.

"Did you have much rain Monday night? It simply poured here; we had 303 points overnight and of course it put the creek up. Bob Pereira was here for tea Tuesday night and said the road at the creek was covered with scores of crayfish which had come down with the creek."

Shifting to Cumnock Farm

I do not have any clear memories of the actual shifting perhaps because it was six decades ago; and also because George offered to come for a week and help with the heavy lifting I was not writing letters to him, so I don't have any to draw on for information. We do have George's daily diaries he kept at the time and which, though not detailed, do give some idea of what happened. Old letters and diaries are such an amazing source of history.

George's Diary:

Saturday 10th January: *Got load of firewood. Carted one load of super. Went over to Beryl's to stay a week and help with shifting.*

Sunday 11th January: *Spent morning with Beryl. Took services at Cowra Rd and Greenethorpe.* (typical!)

Monday 12th January: *Uncle Alf and I took a load of boxes over to new farm and laid lino in kitchen. Beryl came with us and we went round sheep.* (Presumably I made myself useful and cleaned or did something more than just have a ride around the sheep.)

Tuesday 13th January: *Aunty Mavis came with us and polished floors.* (Probably they took another load of something over.)

Wednesday 14th January: *Spent night in new place. Frank Gray helped carry a load of furniture.*

Thursday 15th January: *Frank and Ernest helped and we carried two loads of furniture including the piano.*

Friday 16th January: *Took cows from Spring Vale to Cumnock Farm and got another load.*

Saturday 17th January: *Carted two loads of things from back yard and garage. Ernest found Barney last night much to Beryl's relief.* (and how)

Sunday 18th January: *We had a quiet day at Cumnock Farm. Went to Presbyterian Church Service in Weddin Hall at 3pm. Mr Thomas preached on 'Look after the roots.' Uncle Alf drove us around the farm. Early to bed.*

Monday 19th January: *Helped unload truck. Then helped put on part load at Merrilea before coming home to Watta.*

My letters to George:

Tuesday 20th January: *"I very nearly scribbled the usual RMB 437 etc at the top of the page—probably it will take me a little time to become quite accustomed to my new address. We are gradually getting things to rights, and of course when the sale is over we will be able to find homes for many more things and settle in properly.*

"Do you remember Uncle Frank telling us of a Border Collie pup whose small young owner was reluctant to part with? Well, Dad persuaded them that the puppy would be much better on a farm and it is to be ours on Friday. What do you think of that?"

Thursday 22nd January: "We haven't seen sight nor sign of Whitenose, but all the other cats are doing fine and Kitty Quarmby's behaviour is beyond reproach. Poor Barney won't leave the house unless forcibly put out the door, and then marches around the house to go and sit in my bedroom window and ask to be let in. He is tricked here; can't open the doors and let himself in and out as he used to do at Merrilea. He seems quite happy though, and we intend to get him used to the sheds and surroundings in time."

Friday 23rd January: "I went to town with Dad today and we collected our little Border Collie pup called Tinker and he is a real darling. He sat on the seat between dad and I coming home and was perfectly good. He thinks it is great to have a lamb to practise his art on and has a lovely time keeping it and Snidey the cat wherever he thinks they should stay till he thinks fit to let them go. Elaine gets disgusted and rescues her precious 'Fido' before too long."

(More about Tinker on the 14th February: "This afternoon after afternoon tea, we got in the ewes and lambs and Dad crutched over thirty of them—that will be the next job to do I guess. The lambs are lovely big fellows and look A1. Tinker already has more sense than most grown up dogs; he just loves his work and is going to be exceptionally good if he keeps on the way he is going now.")

Spending time with Tinker the
day before my wedding.

Tuesday 27th January, the day before Gibb's clearing sale: *"Another beautiful big bunch of carnations is before me on the table and their perfume is glorious. Mr Gibb gave them to us yesterday with another cucumber and some tomatoes. The peaches are ripe now and we are enjoying them very much indeed.*

"Mr. And Mrs. Gibb are coming out about 7am tomorrow so I will have to get myself out of bed a little earlier than I have been. They are going to have dinner with us; it won't be an easy day for them and we can at least help that way."

29th January, after the sale: *"I guess you would like to know how the sale day went for us. We had a very busy day really; Mr. and Mrs. Gibb were out early and there was all their furniture and goods to take* out. I did some extra cooking and just as well as we had three sittings for afternoon tea. Peter called in about 1pm. Next came Aunty Pearl, Betty and Joyce, then we asked Mrs Knight in as she was roasting in their lorry all by herself. After a while Uncle Sam and Aunty Lizzie came; followed by Les who was in turn followed by his parents who came looking for him!

"Then, of course Uncles Arthur and Frank, Mr and Mrs Gibb and Dad were all in for a 'cuppa', so things were kept moving. Pearl and Frank stayed and had tea with us after the sale. Our house is just about filled with flowers; Mr and Mrs Gibb brought us some, Aunty Betty sent some and Aunty Pearl arrived with a lovely bunch and they all made the place look so much nicer. There are seven bunches in the dining room, one in Mum's bedroom, one in the porch and two in the kitchen; we had fun trying to find some vases and jars to hold them all.

"Mr and Mrs Gibb, Peter and others have been so thoughtful in giving us vegetables and tomatoes. At the moment we have stacks of tomatoes so we may eat as many as we want. Even Barney had tomatoes and bread and butter for his breakfast today.

"We had a surprise visit from Pa, Aunty Mavis, Clarrie, Al and Ernest this afternoon and they stayed till after six and were very interested to see the new home and property. Ernest was very anxious lest Barney should have a grudge against him as he was the one who found him on 16th Jan. and presumably kept him securely in a box till he could be taken to Cumnock Farm the next day; but Barney condescended to be very gracious and gladly ate the sparrow Ernest gave him; caught in the Lyceum (shearer's hut).

"We are all feeling rather tired, it was hard to settle down last night; poor Dad didn't go to sleep until 3am, then people were coming with their lorries and what have you for their purchases before 5am, and from then on.

"We don't have Kitty Quarmby with us now. Her 'parents' came late this afternoon and collected her. We will miss her after having her with us four weeks. She was a dear little thing and so good."

Monday, 2nd February 1953, after buying Cumnock Farm: "We have had another busy day, the washing in the morning, then I *knitted for a while, and when it was cooler, decided to blacklead and polish the kitchen stove; then silverfrost the sides and back and finished up by scrubbing the surrounding brickwork and hearth. I'm very pleased with the result; it looks much brighter and cleaner. Then, that not being enough for one day, I scrubbed all the verandah and when that was done to my satisfaction, I turned land girl and went and helped Dad with some sheep. I should be well and truly trained by the time you get me George, but at present I'm quite unused to sheep and these <u>were</u> very <u>big</u> ones and rather wild or lively, I don't know which; so I kept close to Dad and hoped for the best. A few of the sheep had pinkeye and I had to put the drops in while Dad held the sheep. I didn't mind really and it was a help to Dad. That over I turned gardener (a versatile girl) and watered the vegetables until it was dark and I was called in for tea. The garden is doing very well, the beans are flowering so it won't be long before we have some of our own vegetables."*

Tuesday 10th February: *"I have been occupied quite a part of the day carting out kurrajong leaves and grass to make a compost heap, but haven't even done a quarter of the job, but what I have done looks considerably better for the clean-up.*

"Elaine and I had to try our hands at yet another farm job this afternoon—unloading superphosphate. Needless to say we didn't lift any; I just couldn't, and could hardly see how anyone can, but we pushed the bags over near Dad for him to carry them from the lorry into the shed. We had the sheep in again yesterday, one has footrot, but those we were treating for pinkeye are responding very well."

Wednesday 11th February: *"Things are going along quite well here, although we had a diversion this morning which we could have managed without quite nicely. Just about 11.30 I was raking more leaves with Tinker's assistance when Mum came out to give Eve, the tiny lamb, a bottle but a quick search revealed no lambie; but on going up to the other end of the little yard, Mum thought she heard a faint bleat and there sure enough was the poor little thing down the well. By then Dad had just arrived home with another load of poles and I ran down to where he was.*

He quickly got a rope and came up; then making a lasso of it and leaning down over the opening to the well, waited till the lamb swam round and lassood it round the neck and pulled it up. I'm sure I didn't know what we would have done if Dad hadn't been there. Poor little thing, it did look cold, wet and forlorn when we fished it out but seems to have recovered from its unpleasant ordeal quite well.

"Dad brought the wheat and oats over this afternoon and we helped him unload them too. That is everything over here now; Dad just has to take the lorry back in the morning and that will be the end of that. He is glad it is over as he wants to get on with ploughing the orchard, mowing the burrs and the rest of the farm work that needs doing."

Friday 13th February: "I fished out some music this morning and had a little practice; half an hour or so. I had expected my fingers to be terribly stiff and unmanageable but they obeyed the messages from my brain quite well and I enjoyed my little while back at the piano again. I had missed it very much really; in spite of the long breaks I have had from it all, music is really an indispensable part of my make up."

Wednesday 18th February: "We are busy crutching—at least Dad is doing the actual crutching and Elaine and I are taking it in turns to help with the mustering, yarding and penning up, picking up and sorting the wool etc and helping Mum indoors; so what with one thing and another we are all going flat out and are pretty tired when the day is over."

Time in Sydney for holiday and shopping, 23rd February—7th March 1953

George had mentioned the possibility of having a break of a week or more in Sydney after all the work involved in moving; sometime late January or early February. In a letter to George dated 10th February I wrote: "Yes, darling I expect I will be able to go with you and we were wondering if you would take Elaine down for a visit with the Jackson's; she needs the change and it is a good opportunity."

Mum had been doing some more thinking and wrote to a Mrs Glad Fergusson, who she felt would be a good person to shepherd me around the Sydney shops while looking for material for the wedding dress and bridesmaids' gowns, and anything else I may have wanted to shop for. She was right there. So after a few starts and stops regarding accommodation, Elaine and I caught the train on the afternoon of Monday, 23rd February, getting off at Wattamondara, the first stage of our holiday.

We left for Sydney the next morning about 7.15am, having a picnic lunch at Katoomba and after a good trip arriving at George's Aunty Meg and Uncle Ron Hewitt's at Bondi Junction at 3.15pm. Later we drove to the Jackson's home at Brighton-le-Sands, having the evening meal with them, leaving Elaine and returning to Bondi Junction.

This was the time of the Annual Methodist conference and as part of this three big public Demonstrations were held in the Sydney Town Hall, always well-attended. George had written and booked five seats for the Young People's Demonstration which was on next day. His diary says: *"We drove into the city and collected the tickets and met Jackson's and Elaine outside the Town Hall and went to the Y.P. Demo. together."* One of the big features of these was the fabulous Crusader Choir with several hundred young voices, worth going a long way to hear. We had a wonderful evening.

On Thursday 26th February we visited George's mother's friends, Mr and Mrs Potter at Willoughby and stopped for tea. They wrote to George's Mum saying we were the loveliest couple they had ever met. Strangely now we have no memory of them or our visit. That night we went to the Overseas Missions Demonstration in the Town Hall and particularly enjoyed an address by Lazarus Lami Lami, a lovable native from one of the Mission fields.

Friday 27th February, we went out to Jacksons then to Aunty Stella who lived at Rockdale quite close by, and had lunch with her and Aunty Alice Litt who must have come from her home at Wentworthville to have some time with us. We drove the two aunts to the City and "looked round the Museum for an hour or so".

Saturday 28th February: Margaret, who was a nurse at Waverley Methodist War Memorial Hospital, had a day off so we picked her up and went for a drive up along the northern beaches to Palm Beach and back again through Kuringai; a pleasant day.

Sunday 1st March was a quiet day, and Aunty Meg, George and I went to church at night.

Monday 2nd March: George took me out to Fergusson's at Rockdale in the afternoon, staying for tea and after that it was all go for me for the next four days.

Tuesday 3rd March: I started my shopping under Mrs Fergusson's guidance. I bought my going away dress at a little boutique; the skirt needed shortening so we had that attended to and went back another day to pick it up. I don't remember whether I bought my handbag and shoes or waited till home again, probably the latter.

That night George met Elaine and I outside the Empire Theatre and we saw the show 'White Horse Inn' and all enjoyed it immensely.

The next day I guess I did more looking and thinking. George had tea with us at Rockdale and the following day, Thursday 5th March, I bought the materials for my bridal gown and the bridesmaids at a place called Leonards. I wanted my maids to wear apricot and the only way to achieve that effect was to have light apricot organza over pink grosgrain which worked well.

George and I met and had lunch together at David Jones and in the afternoon went to the Home Missions Demonstration. George's diary on Friday 6th March records that he went shopping with me, Elaine and Mrs Fergusson and that Margaret joined us in the afternoon. That would have been when we to Browns the

Milliners to choose which shapes, to be covered later, suited the two bridesmaids best. That done, we probably bought the gloves they would wear too.

That night we went to Aunty Meg's for tea, had some music with me at the piano and Uncle Ron playing his violin. George and I then went to Fergusson's to be ready to leave for home in the morning. We left there about 7.15am, picked up Elaine and came home via Goulburn, arriving at Cumnock Farm about 6pm.

Sunday 8th March: George records he slept in late (good idea), also that he finished his sermon, (he had spent nearly all Tuesday working on it), that we spent most of the day together, and that he took the service at Grenfell that night—that's my George. He probably went back to Pontefract Park that night.

Cumnock Farm, March 1953

Letters to George, 10th March: *"We took Fluff back to her parents yesterday before going to dressmaking. Mum made some tomato and pineapple jam yesterday with two jars for you and me. I carted out three more loads of leaves and grass this afternoon and estimate there are about twelve to go!"*

Friday 13th March: *"I think we will be going to Merrilea tomorrow afternoon to collect the gladioli corms; they should be ready now."*

Tuesday 17th March: *"I opened the roll of my wedding dress material today to have a look at the lace, which I knew would be on top. Mum and Dad loved it and dad said he can hardly wait for the wedding to see it now. I can't either, I'm getting awfully excited already George, after all, only about 25 weeks now. It doesn't sound that long when you put it that way."*

Saturday 21st March: *"George and all his family had their first visit to Cumnock Farm for tea and the evening. Enjoyed time together."*

Wednesday 25th March: *"Did Dad tell you he has put in an order for a Ferguson tractor? Of course we here are not surprised; he has* been able to think and talk of little else for weeks and it will be best for him to get it now and done with, there are so many jobs to be done that need a tractor."

Tuesday 29th March: *"Allan and Thelma Fenton and family came out this afternoon for some figs and grapes to make jam. Also Uncle Sam, Aunty Liz and Mrs Hewson, a friend and ex-Grenfellite, came for the run and I presume, to see us. They stayed till 6.30 and it is now nearly eight. When the fruit picking was over and the rest of us came inside, the kiddies stayed out and had a grand time giving each other rides in the wood cart, with Tinker and the two lambs prancing alongside enjoying themselves hugely too. They thought it was just lovely having the children to play with them."*

Dressmaking—29th: *"I was very good this week; I did my model. It is awfully cute, you should see it, a dress for a six year old girl. It is really funny—the last two weeks Grace has had us 2nd years on children's drafts and Colleen and Laurel say that it must be for my benefit—they won't be needing them for many a long day. By the time I need them, if ever, I am certain I'll have forgotten all about them in all probability."*

Elaine and I had been asked if we would help in the Grenfell Sunday School Kindergarten and on the 29th I wrote: *"I have had my first shot at kindergarten teaching and quite enjoyed it. You should see me on a kindergarten chair!"*

31st March: *"Elaine and I spent all this morning and a little while this afternoon helping Dad muster and draft the wethers. We have them in two mobs now, one of 600 for us to keep and one of 164 to sell if we can. I like helping with the sheep and it was a lovely morning apart from the dust. I felt filthy when it was over as my particular job kept me in a position where the dust blew all over me and I couldn't very well dodge it."*

Easter was approaching and the Crusader Camp was at Young again, where I had attended my first five years previously. On the 31st March I wrote to George: *"My study book and programme came in the mail today, also a note from Rev. Parsons asking if I will be prepared to lead or assist lead a study circle. I don't altogether like the idea,* and I had said I was going to stay absolutely free from any responsibility this camp. Surely they can't be <u>that</u> badly off for leaders."

Needless to say George didn't escape responsibility. In his diary Thursday 2nd April he noted that he was Transport Officer and a study circle leader.

Some people used to refer to Crusader Camps as matrimonial bureaus. They were much, much more, but many people did meet their future wives and husbands at them—George and I among them. If we (plus my Dad) had not both been at Canberra at Easter 1951, it is very doubtful that we would have met each other elsewhere.

Farewell

The Cowra Road folk planned to give us a farewell evening on 10th April. In a letter to George two days before I told him at length how we were all dreading it but in another letter two days after the occasion I wrote that: *"we not only survived but quite enjoyed it although there was naturally some strain. They didn't make us walk in to "For they are jolly good fellows" or anything like that; and we didn't even have to sit up in front of everyone while the speeches were on; it was very thoughtful of them. The evening was just from the church and club folk; there were forty or so there, and the evening passed away very happily with competitions, salmagundi and speeches (very nice ones incidentally) then supper. It was quite late when we arrived home, after 1am. PS. A lot of people at the farewell asked after you and wanted to know why you weren't there."*

12th April: I started on a jumper for George, noting it would be interesting to see if I could do the pattern when I got up that far. The only thing I can remember knitting him was a sleeveless blue pullover.

20th April: *"I plucked up my courage and asked Grace Hunter if she would make my wedding dress and the bridesmaids' dresses and to my relief and elation she said yes. During the May holidays she is going out to Waverley War Memorial Hospital to see Ila and will take Margaret's measurements then, so that is another problem solved."*

But on 25th April I wrote to George that Grace now felt she didn't have the time to do the actual sewing but was prepared to help draft the patterns and cut out the dresses. We asked our close neighbours Alice and Shirley Simpson and they agreed to do the sewing, sometimes assisted by their sister Ellen. (PS. In due course Alice married Bruce Robinson and Shirley married John Best.)

Thursday 30th April: *"Dad and I went out to Thelma and Allan Fenton's today to collect a plough or something Dad is borrowing. He expects his tractor to arrive Saturday. Sam and 'Blos' were there too and I had a nice chat and cup of tea with them while Dad was getting the 'dope' from Allan."*

6th May: *"Dad's tractor arrived today and he just can't wait to try it out and get the ground prepared for the lucerne and it planted. He ordered a scoop too but it hasn't arrived yet. He sold some of the sheep we picked out to sell, on Saturday and the rest today, at a nice profit too. We have had 125 points of rain and still raining."*

Tuesday 9th June: *"I made a little progress on my dressing gown. Grace won't be coming for the weekend now but suggested yesterday that we could come in this afternoon at two and work on the dresses, which we did. I started on the foundation drafts last night; then we continued with them this afternoon and have the patterns all cut out ready to cut out the dresses except for Margaret's shirt, my skirt and train and slip bodice. I will do those through the week and then we will start cutting out the dresses next Tuesday, all being well. It's all most exciting, isn't it?"*

Thursday 11th June: *"I spent most of yesterday afternoon doing drafts and all this afternoon on the dressing gown—there is certainly some work in it, the biggest job I have tackled yet."*

22nd June: *"One of the things I have been doing is helping Dad unload the bricks, remembering of course your instructions and not* attempting to lift any of the ten brick blocks. I concentrate on the single bricks and one in each hand is quite enough for me."

Tuesday 23rd June: *"I was in town all this afternoon again getting the bridesmaid's underdresses cut out, it should only take one more afternoon to finish up now, thank goodness. Grace offered to help with the bridesmaid's hats, to pin them up and then we will be able to go on from there, so that's another little problem solved."*

30th June: *"We have Fluff Quarmby with us again. Mr Quarmby took Mrs Quarmby down to Sydney to see a specialist. Fluff rode home all the way from church on my lap, was very well behaved and settled in well as we expected she would."*

Tuesday 4th August: *"Fluff protested loudly all the way into town yesterday; she didn't want to go home a bit. When it was time to leave, I had to go down to the shed and take her away from the mouse hole she was contentedly watching. She will have to resign herself to being a town cat once again."*

Thursday 2nd July: *"Thelma and Lizzie are supposed to be coming out tomorrow to cut out the curtains and help us a little with making them. I hope nothing happens to prevent them coming this time. It will be lovely to have it done.*

"I had the first fitting of my wedding dress today, nothing very much to see yet of course, but everything is going along well. Elaine had a fitting too; we can hardly wait to see the dresses in one piece and nearing completion—Patience Beryl, patience! I'm loving doing this white satin set and am sick to death of the pink gown. If I was sensible and worked on it for a couple of hours I'd have it almost finished, so I'll have to give myself a talking to and get it done."

5th July: *"Elaine and I had another fitting of our dresses this morning and they are looking lovely, Elaine was terribly excited and thrilled. In a week or two more mine should be looking more as the finished garment is meant to be. The Rector says we can have the Anglican Hall for the reception."*

Visitors, dresses, and wedding preparations

21st July: *"Aunty Mavis and Pa came for lunch today and spent the afternoon with us. The time went very quickly and we had a lovely time together. Aunty Mavis brought me another present; an extremely dainty crocheted jug cover; it is sweet. Pa was in high spirits, making funny remarks about my cooking and wanting to know how my wedding dress was coming along, if it had a train etc. He has always been interested in dress, used to have some input into what his wife wore; most of her dresses were made by a dressmaker and his preference was for bright florals on a darker background. I remember once I was knitting a short sleeved jumper in 2-ply wool with a lacy pattern; with a twinkle in in his hazel eyes he asked me why I was knitting something to keep me warm when it was mostly holes! They also brought us some cuttings for the garden."*

24th July: *"We had a nice visit from Stan and Brenda Pfeiffer. I was doing a little to my white satin nightgown and Brenda wanted to know if it was my wedding dress!—as if I would be working on it in front of them? Dot put up the hem for me and it is all done now ready for the lace when I find a suitable one nice enough.*

"There is a registered parcel waiting for me at the Post Office so I'm hoping it is from Leonards. All the tucks in the bridesmaid's dresses had used a lot of material and I had to send away for more.

"We left home at 9.30 this morning and I had a big day shopping at Young. We spent approximately three hours in Miss Dorrington's shop and came home with some lovely hats and suits on approval, and were highly entertained all the time we were there—she is terribly funny."

Note: Miss Dorrington was Bruce Brown's Aunt and had a shop packed to the ceiling with cardboard boxes with all her goods packed away in them with lots of tissue paper. No one was allowed to help get them down or pack away again; shopping time was a unique experience. I bought my 'going away' hat there and the wax orange blossom tiara.

25th July: *"The parcel was the material I ordered in the first place from Leonards so that is quite a relief. We are going in again tomorrow to have another go at cutting out the skirts and if we are able to whittle down the number of yards we need in addition, I will be glad.*

"You will <u>have</u> to come over this weekend darling; Mrs Hocking is expecting you for dinner. She rang up Sunday morning to ask if we could come for dinner, but she wanted to know if you were here too and said several times—'I do want that young man', so we put it off to this coming weekend, assuming you would be coming over again. She calls you—'the smiling young man'; remember? So you cannot disappoint her, let alone me, can you?

"Yet another present came today; a silver beetroot server from Aunty Stella and Joan Sweeting gave me a nice tea towel when she was here Saturday night. We thoroughly enjoyed Joan and George's visit. Joan wondered if I had any sandwich filling I would particularly like at the wedding breakfast—of course I said asparagus and she said they had already planned to have it and chicken, so as the third we thought perhaps corn beef or something like that would be nice. She brought along the serviettes to show us; she bought them at Cowra recently as there is a better choice there, and they are lovely."

28th July: *"We have both skirts cut out now apart from the extra pieces we have to let in. We have brought the eleven yards down to eight. That will be ample so I must get a letter away asking for this tomorrow. All will soon be done now I'm thankful to say.*

"Mr Cramb offered Dad the loan of their lorry and Peter this afternoon to go out to the mill on the Bimbi Road and get a load of scantlings. The mill owners are glad to give them away and only burn them otherwise. Dad obtained some pieces he is going to make into gates, others he is going to saw to make grating for the holding yards of the shearing shed, and others to make slats for the wool table". The wool table is still being used nearly 60 years later.

6th August: *"We got onto the guest list again working out the number of invitations needed. We have had a most beautiful 136 points of rain this morning."*

13th August: George and I bought our bedroom suite and mattress at Cowra and also saw Mrs Hutchinson about flowers for the wedding bouquets. Later George took her samples of the dress materials.

15th August: Mum, Dad and Elaine came over to have a look at the cottage that will be my home. After the evening meal George and I had two games of checkers.

[There's always been a cat: Jon]

25th July 1953: *"Poor Jon has been in the wars. There has been a stray cat around, and one night Jon appeared with minor scratches and a swollen and closed eye, the result of an encounter with the said cat, we presume. Then last night after an absence of a day or more he reappeared with a terribly swollen and cut paw in addition to his former afflictions. He told us a very long story all about it and we gave him a big meal and today he has been looking after himself, sitting in the sun."*

Tuesday 4th August: *"It isn't very often that one would be overjoyed to be awakened at 5am on an August morning by someone at the window is it; but Elaine and I were thrilled to hear a familiar voice at my window this morning. Yes, it was Jon whom we hadn't had sight nor sign of for four days. I hopped out of the window (quite a sight to behold I assure you), picked him up and a very happy Jon spent what remained of the night on my bed. It is lovely to have him back; he has a place all his own in our hearts and we were beginning to wonder if anything had happened to him. His foot is still extremely sore and one big hole in particular is still very nasty but the swelling has gone down considerably. Snidey is very pleased to see him again also and they spent the day together in the pram."*

Wedding preparations continue

4th August: *"Mum had a ring from Aunty Mavis a little while ago asking if Friday, 21st of this month will be free for us; the Cowra Road folk want to give me a gift evening that night. Isn't it lovely of them? Anyway we said yes, it would suit so I hope it is right with you, too beloved. You will just <u>have</u> to come too, you know.*

"I had another fitting of my dress today and it continues to progress well. We took up the hem today. Mum came with us to see it and she is very satisfied also. Have you heard from Margaret when she will be coming up? We were wondering today when it will be."

6th August: *"This time next week we will be together once again darling, won't that be lovely? I am quite excited about it and am becoming <u>ENORMOUSLY</u> excited at the thought of our wedding."*

7th August: *"Elaine and I spent all morning helping Dad saw timber and wood. We have had 136 points of rain during the first week of August; a wonderful rain."*

9th August: *"Planning our home is a very real thrill, isn't it? I do believe I am the happiest and luckiest girl in the whole wide world; having you and sharing such love, trust and understanding, our faith in God, and having such a dear little home awaiting us; aren't we a fortunate pair?"*

10th August: *"We had a wonderful time with the Grays; you would have thought it was only last week we last saw Edith instead of ten months ago at her wedding. We four girls sat on our beds just as we always did and talked and talked; we had such a lot to tell each other and hear about.*

"Mr & Mrs Campbell Diprose came to see us last night. They were very interested in seeing round the place and after tea we had a nice talk and sing-song. Mr Diprose loves music and Elaine and I played several duets and I also had to play his 'special' on the organ—'Sweet Hour of Prayer'. When I was organist at Cowra Road, he would ask me to include it in the music as frequently as I could.

"He was teasing me a little and expressing surprise that our love affair still continued when you had to come twice as far to see me. He didn't think

you would think me worth it, but I assured him you probably believed the old proverb that 'A bird in the hand is worth two in the bush!'"

11th August: *"Grace came as expected Saturday and we enjoyed having her very much. Saturday night she pinned up the bridesmaids' hats and while I sewed on one layer of material, she went on pinning the next and now I have just one layer to sew on each, and they will be done apart from any flower we may decide on and a band of buckram inside it."*

Monday 17th August: *"Something so very exciting happened today, the girls gave a luncheon in my honour and presented me with a lovely bunch of jonquils and carnations, and a pair of beautiful towels with their good wishes for my future happiness. Wasn't that absolutely wonderful of them? It was a complete surprise; I was completely engrossed in a new type of draft I was doing, not noticing what the girls were doing, when Marie said 'Beryl, do you know this luncheon is for you?' They had set the long tables with tablecloths and in case you are interested in 'eats', (and what men aren't) we had bread rolls, tinned ham, corned beef, tomatoes, jellied beetroot, lettuce, sliced eggs and mayonnaise, lemon cheese tartlets made by Marie and iced cake made by Julie. I am the first of the dressmaking class to get married and the girls thought it called for a celebration. It was a lovely celebration and there was quite a lot of speculation as to whom the next would be. Some of the girls have been going for four years and this is the first time one has left classes to be married; so it seems as though I am making history."*

My Kitchen Tea—Spring Vale Shearing Shed—Thursday, 20th August

Writing on the 17th, with reference to the coming kitchen tea, I said, *"I am looking forward to all the evening except the speeches and first coming into the shed. I will go to Spring Vale when I get there, so you can come to the house too and we can wait there where it is warm and comfortable, and when we know they are ready make our entry."*

We arrived to the singing of '*for she's a jolly good fellow*', and little cousin Gwenda Pereira presented me with a bouquet. The evening was spent with games, competitions, speeches to which George and I both replied, and supper was served, before "*a very enjoyable and memorable evening came to a close.*" (*The Grenfell Record*)

We received a lot of useful and lovely gifts, including an egg beater from Ron and Sadie Diprose which I am still using.

1st September: "*Dad finished fixing up the shed this afternoon and we got in the ewes and lambs to sort them out from the others. He is going to go on shearing the lambs to get them out of the way before the fun begins in earnest next week. I guess it will be Elaine or I for it as shed hand in the morning.*"

Saturday 5th September: "*In the afternoon we went to have the weekend with Ken Ward who is going to be our groomsman and has been a good friend to us both since Crusader camp days and lived with his parents on the family farm, 'Winona', Frampton south of Cootamundra. We had a pleasant, relaxing time and left Monday morning. We lunched at Young, bought the wedding ring and bridesmaids' gifts—a string of pearls, and going on to Grenfell, bought the linoleum for our bedroom; a lovely one of trailing wine coloured roses on a light fawn base.*"

Wednesday 9th September: "*Elaine is opposite me sealing the last of the wedding invitation envelopes. With almost sixty to do, she is not licking them but using a saucer of water and cotton wool.*

"*The last two days have been very busy. I have just about made up for the long weekend I had away. Yesterday we washed then in the afternoon scrubbed the side and front verandahs and back porch and laundry and then polished the kitchen—all this apart from the lunches and a little gardening and the usual routine work.*

"*This morning Mum and I decided to take advantage of the lovely weather and wash some sheets, pillowslips, towels and tea towels; which we duly did. We thought it would be easier to do it here where we have the washing machine to do the work. We did three pairs of sheets, six pillowslips, eight towels and seven tea towels; so that is a start for us as we set up house. I will iron the sheets, pillowslips and tea towels tomorrow.*

"This morning Elaine and I spent some time mustering sheep to help Dad and this afternoon I finished putting lace around the neck of my nightgown; then pressed all my fancywork with a damp cloth and hot iron; this last job taking a lot of time, believe you me.

"Our shearing is progressing well and we are pleased with Mr Hardy who is a very good shearer, good tempered and pleasant to work with. We start the wethers tomorrow, the ewes and lambs are all done.

"I haven't had any word about the dresses since I came home so am just hoping they have been able to get the diamante and that the three dresses are almost finished. I am getting to the stage that I want to see them complete."

Saurday 12th September: *"Eva Myers is coming out with us after church tomorrow to stay till Monday morning. She is one of the very nicest girls there is.*

"Dad baled up wool this afternoon and we have fourteen bales now and about three more still to do."

Tuesday 15th September: *"Elaine and I had another late night last night and didn't get home till eleven thirty. We went down to Simpson's for another fitting—Elaine was beside herself with excitement; it was the first time she had tried her dress on. They are all really highly successful and should be finished by next Saturday, though mine may be a few days longer as we had to send away for more diamante and they may take a little time to get here. The evening really flew; we were all busy the entire time and we had a lovely evening.*

"The dressmaking girls are coming out Thursday afternoon, also Shirley and Alice Simpson and Helen I'anson, so you will be able to imagine me that afternoon sitting up and playing hostess to a dozen or so girls. Elaine made two cakes this afternoon and tomorrow I will have to hope I am in the mood for cooking, don my white apron and see what I can do.

"*By the way, the first acceptance came in the mail today from the Campbell Diproses.*

"*On Sunday afternoon Sam, Lizzie, Roma, Wilbur and Richard came out to see my things.*"

It was the custom back then to display the contents of one's 'glory box'—'hope chest', call it what you like—to friends before one married. The women were supposed to be responsible for the household linen, sheets, pillowslips, tea towels, tablecloths, towels and bits and pieces such as fancywork. If a pair of soft white towels appeared, knowing looks would be exchanged with perhaps a few remarks of the "Now I wonder who these are for," variety.

I think it was my Mother who gave me a pair and sure enough they were being used before we celebrated our first wedding anniversary. What with gifts given over the years, 21st birthday presents, the Kitchen Tea given by Grenfell and Cowra Road friends and relations, I already had a very good supply of useful and ornamental articles.

Mum paid a local lady to embroider a lovely big supper cloth with roses in pink and deep red tones. I haven't used it yet; I think it would be great as a wall hanging. It came with half a dozen serviettes with a rosebud in one corner. I paid Marie Mackey to embroider the rosebuds and Betty Graham to crochet the edges a few years ago.

I didn't get carried away doing lots of 'fancy work' for my 'box', but I did enjoy doing a few pieces including two little mats for which I actually did the crochet edge and two duchess sets. One was with gold and orange poppies, the other with pansies in ecru tone which I later gave to my daughter Jeanette. I also did a duchess set of four pieces—one large mat and three smaller ones, in blue cross stitch outlined in dark blue back stitch. I love that set and have used it quite a lot. The last was a table centre done mostly in buttonhole stitch and cross and stem stitch. The lovely crochet edges on these last two were done by my friend

Mrs Gertie Jackson. The table centre actually won 1st prize in the Greenethorpe Show!

On reading that, don't you dare think to yourself, "There probably wouldn't be much competition in small communities such as Greenethorpe". They were the very places where pride entered and all did their very best to ensure 'their' show had an excellent display.

Tuesday 22nd September: *"Elaine and I went down to Simpson's again last night and it wasn't late this time. The dresses are certainly beautiful; Elaine and Margaret's will be completed in a day or two and we are waiting for 15 dozen more diamante for mine. Once they arrive it will be finished in a day or so too and we are hoping they soon are here.*

"Aunty Pearl, Uncle Frank, Joyce and Glad and Ralph Fergusson were here for the afternoon and Mum and Dad were pleased to meet Glad and Ralph again and we had a nice afternoon here as we know they are unable to come to the wedding.

"We have received word that ninety five are coming now, that is apart from eleven at the bridal table but 157 were invited and only twenty have let us know they are unable to come."

Monday 28th September: *"We had a trip out to Quandialla and picked up Aunty Dot and Uncle Arthur who were 'waiting at the church' surrounded by boxes and luggage. Dad and Arthur spent practically the entire day in the garden and they certainly made a difference to it."*

Aunty Dot would have been a big help to Mum in the days leading up to the wedding.

Our Wedding Day
3rd October, 1953

The long awaited day arrived at last! I woke early and climbed out my bedroom window so as not to disturb the others in the house. I walked around the garden and decided we were going to have a lovely, warm spring day for our wedding.

During the morning, George arrived bringing Margaret and the bride's and bridesmaids' bouquets from the florist, Mrs Hutchison in Cowra. My flowers were lovely; gladioli, orchids and touches of sweet peas, blue forget-me-not and very fine maiden hair fern, backed by tulle.

I guess we had some kind of lunch; all I remember is banana custard. By a coincidence that was what George's mother served him too!

With the ceremony timed to start at 2pm, we needed to keep an eye on the clock. In those far off days there was no thought of employing professionals for manicures, makeup and hair dos. We checked our hands and if the nails were nicely shaped and clean, that was it. Hair wasn't a problem either; Elaine's was naturally curly, Margaret wore hers in a plait wound around her head and I would have washed and set mine the previous day if I wanted to. Make up would have been simple too. I don't think I possessed more than powder and two or three choices of lipstick.

So we made ourselves ready. I don't think there were any dramas, I just felt relaxed and happy. After having two or three photos taken, off we went, I in a black 1948 Chevrolet driven and owned by my Grandfather. There were more photographs on our arrival at the church, which had been beautifully decorated with flowers by our church friends.

At last, I walked up the church's left porch steps, and down the aisle on my proud Father's arm to my waiting bridegroom.

Grandpa waits to drive Beryl to the wedding.

George and Beryl Walker.

George, Beryl, Stan Walker, Elaine Pereira,
Ken Ward and Margaret Walker.

Beryl Walker.